Words of

Peace and
Protection

DEVOTIONS FOR WOMEN

CONCORDIA PUBLISHING HOUSE · SAINT LOUIS

1 2 3 4 5 6 7 8 9 10   31 30 29 28 27 26 25 24 23 22

CONTENTS

To the Reader

The first time I heard someone say the words "shelter in place," I was preparing to leave my office for an indeterminate length of time. I packed my computer, reference books, and favorite pen so I could work from home. Then I felt dread; what if I never came back? I cleaned out my office, removing personal items and preparing for someone else to handle what I couldn't carry out that day.

It was the beginning of the global shutdown caused by efforts to stall the coronavirus pandemic. For the next few months, many of us stayed home. We stockpiled nonperishable food and paper products. We put on masks. We kept our distance from others.

During that time, I spent more time outdoors, developed a fondness for jigsaw puzzles, and watched church online. I also discovered virtual choral and music productions. You may have seen them too—people performing by themselves but joining others in video compilations for what are, in effect, concerts. Although I can't sing (not even a little), I even participated in one as a tribute to a friend who was retiring.

After a few weeks, I went back to work in the office, consumed the stockpiled goods, and took off my mask. But I still watch those videos. They give me a keen appreciation for the individual voice among a chorus of others.

That's what this book is. It's a collection of fifty-two voices—individuals who contribute their own experience and wisdom and inspiration to blend into one song. But not just any song. This book is a concert inspired by a psalm.

Psalm 91 is a beautiful song about sheltering in place, hunkering down under the protection and peace and love of our almighty God. When the world rages and we need to take cover, God provides a safe place. When we are weary or frightened, God wraps us in His care. When we feel fretful, apprehensive, discomforted, our heavenly Father comforts us, calms us, and reassures us. And when we are feeling strong and brave, rejoicing in all the good things life can offer, our Lord is with us then, too, with the perfect grace and love that only He can provide.

Bad things will continue to happen. But wherever you are in your life and whatever life is throwing at you right now, I encourage you to shelter with our Lord in His Word and abide in His Sacraments. He loves you, provides for you, delivers you from evil, forgives you, redeems you, restores you.

The Lord your God is in your midst, a mighty One who will save; He will rejoice over you with gladness; He will quiet you by His love; He will exult over you with loud singing. (ZEPHANIAH 3:17)

The Editor

The Soldier's Psalm

S he can almost reach the left side of her head to brush her hair properly. But not quite. She stares in amazement at the nasty cut on her right pinky toe. She never felt it. A year has passed since her head-on car collision. Initially paralyzed after hitting the windshield, her mobility and the nerve endings in her arms and legs have slowly returned. But not all of them. Every day is both a blessing and a battle.

Whether internal or external, combat is something you and I understand. The battles rage over sins that entangle. Opinions that clash. Jobs that end. Relationships that struggle. Addictions that linger. Health that declines. But take heart, fellow soldier.

Psalm 91 is sometimes called "The Soldier's Psalm." As Christ's followers, we understand daily warfare on the spiritual battlefield—both large and small. Some days, we shout for joy when God brings victory. Like when my sister did not die in that car accident. Other days, exhaustion settles in, and we wonder if we have the strength to endure. Like one more day at physical therapy.

God inspired the words of Psalm 91 to provide His children confidence in Him when doubt and weariness face us on the battlefield. On those hard days, God wraps Psalm 91 around our hearts and minds like a protective shield. He reminds us that He has not abandoned us to fight alone or unprotected.

One way to look at this psalm is to read it as though three players interact in it: a believer (vv. 1–2), an audience of encouragers (vv. 3–13), and God (vv. 14–16). Looking at it from this angle, the first two verses provide a humbling example of how to proclaim unwavering trust in God as our shelter and refuge.

This beautiful statement of faith flows from a life thankful for His divine protection! Then comes a homily of encouragement from our fellow soldiers. Only those who have found refuge under God's mighty wings can point to the only place safe from pestilence, terror, and arrows.

When the Lord is our dwelling place, no evil, plague, or darkness ever triumphs. Even though intense battles seem never-ending, we can trust that He will send His angels to stand guard over us. Picturing that truth—actually envisioning that holy guard in our mind—provides the strength we need to stand.

The Soldier's Psalm concludes as God reassures us that He's got this. He's got us. Today, tomorrow, and into eternity, He promises to deliver us from fear and trouble. Refuge awaits all who take shelter under His protective care. All who hold fast to Him in love. All who know His name. When we call on Him, He will answer us, rescue us, and show us His salvation.

Our battles may leave us feeling as if we are lying wounded in the trenches. We may feel paralyzed by fear and doubt. We may stare at a battle wound and wonder how it got there. Every day is both a blessing and a battle. Psalm 91 reassures us that the privilege of taking refuge in the Lord during our battles *is* the blessing.

He who dwells in the shelter of the Most High

will abide in the shadow of the Almighty,

I will say to the LORD, "My refuge and my fortress,

my God, in whom I trust."

PART 1

Psalm 91:1–2

AUTHORS

Deb Burma

Rebekah Curtis

Caitlin May Dinger

Molly Dixon

Sharla Fritz

Perla Gil de Rodriguez

Christina Hergenrader

Martha Streufert Jander

Darcy Paape

Kristina Paul

Sarah Schultz

Covered and Content

Like many children with intense imaginations, I envisioned monsters lurking under my bed. They only attacked when it was dark, so as soon as I switched off the light each night, I bolted toward my bed, then leaped into it so the monsters couldn't snatch me by my feet. Burrowing myself under the canopy of covers, I was safe from danger in my shelter between the sheets, hidden from my imagined enemy. My bed had become my refuge—my place of protection. (Though I didn't dare poke a leg out of my protective canopy!) Resting in the shadow of my covers, I was content to stay put until the light of day, when the monsters went away.

While I have outgrown my fear of imaginary monsters, I face real danger—actual threats against me—and an enemy who attacks in daylight *and* darkness. So do you. But we do not need to fear. Like the psalmist, you and I dwell in the shelter of the Most High. We can run to the Lord and leap into His embrace. Covered in Christ, we are eternally secure—saved from our sins and safe in His grip, now and forever. Our lives are hidden with Christ in God (Colossians 3:3) and nothing can snatch us out of His hand (John 10:28). He is incomparably more powerful than any threat or fear you or I face. Danger may lurk on the outside, but we are inside the Lord's fortress—the protective canopy of His embrace. We find refuge in our God, in whom we trust, and we can be content to stay put—to abide—in His shadow always. He covers us completely.

The almighty, all-powerful God of the universe is, at the same time, so near to you and me that we can envision abiding in His shadow. In Jesus, God came to dwell among us (John 1:14).

Even when we cannot sense the Lord's presence, we trust His perfect promise in Christ: "I am with you always" (Matthew 28:20). He dwells in our hearts through faith (Ephesians 3:17) by the power of the Spirit. Like the psalmist, we call on Him in personal terms: "my refuge . . . my fortress . . . my God," and He hears our every prayer.

We find real shelter in the Lord Most High. His divine protection is all-encompassing, but that doesn't mean we won't face danger or tribulation. Whether monstrous threats come in the form of persecution, illness, temptation, or other trials, we can trust in our God—our refuge—our place of protection. Troubles will come, but we're fortified to face them by the One who has ultimately overcome them (John 16:33) through His death and resurrection. We can be content in every circumstance, trusting God to guard our hearts, keep us in the one true faith, and provide for all our needs in Christ Jesus, our Savior (Philippians 4:6–11).

Sister in Christ, rest contentedly without fear of the future, even when the enemy attacks, the world taunts, or your flesh caves. Trust the Lord for forgiveness; know that He is in control. The Almighty surrounds and defends you. Within His deep, abiding presence, may you know the peace, contentment, and fullness of joy (Psalm 16:11) found only in Christ.

Oh, Stressed the House

A brother of my acquaintance finds joy in referring to the male in-laws of his generation as "paper uncles." The designation stands opposed to his own honored position of "blood uncle." In this way, he seeks to denigrate the husbands of his sisters.

A similar spirit hovers in the 1928 Newbery Medal–winning children's novel *Gay-Neck: The Story of a Pigeon*. A hunter vexed by a belligerent Himalayan water buffalo refers to the animal as a brother-in-law. ("Idiot," the author adds parenthetically, for readers new to the idiom.)

This is just how the guys are talking about each other. By Thumper's Law, I can't repeat what the ladies are saying. There's a reason the houseplant with long, sharp leaves is called a mother-in-law's tongue. Apparently, the daughters-in-law, those sweet things, got naming rights.

Why does this have to be hard?

We'd do best to skip the psychobabble and anthropologizing, and just go straight to sin. You're a sinner, and your in-laws are sinners. Mothers-in-law and daughters-in-law, in particular, may find one another a bit fussy. Showing in-laws charity typically includes an exquisite quality of struggle.

The devil is in the details, so you can fill yours in yourself. But the devil is owed some real credit. He hates stable Christian families because they reveal and confess the love of Christ for His Church and her responsiveness to that love. Satan is an opportunist. He makes the most of the easy target that is generated when a man leaves his father and mother and cleaves to his wife. Dissension among in-laws is simply xenophobia writ small; the normal human suspicion of outsiders transmogrified by mandatory, lifelong propinquity. The sins practically commit themselves!

They don't, though. I am very serious about refusing the intellectual and emotional excuses, disguised as science, that we make for our sins toward in-laws. Is that one "toxic"? Jesus died for him. Does she aggravate your anxiety? Jesus died for her. Do they bring out the worst in you? Confess your sins, not theirs.

Confess your sins and hear this Word: "In the stead and by the command of my Lord Jesus Christ, I forgive you all your sins in the name of the Father and of the Son and of the Holy Spirit."

Jesus died for you.

This doesn't mean you should muscle through it. You can't. Get your head out of your house, and dwell instead in the shelter of the Most High. Abide in the shadow of the Almighty. Say that He is your refuge and your fortress by taking this struggle to the Lord in prayer. The bigger the struggle, the harder that will be to do. The sins you love and hate the most are the ones your flesh will most resist bearing to the throne of grace. But they are too heavy for you. Moreover, they have already been borne to Calvary on the back of the God in whom you trust.

There is just one only-begotten Son. The rest of us are paper sons and paper daughters, written into God's family at the cost of that Son's blood (Ephesians 1:4–7). He called our names in Baptism so they would be written in heaven (Luke 10:20), indelibly entered in the Book of Life (Revelation 3:5). He declares us His own and gives us to each other in marriage, in law, not because we love one person. The gift that begins when two people put their names on one paper is that of learning to love many people.

The Cool Shadow

Walking to church on a warm summer morning, my three boys complain about the sun in their eyes. "It's too bright!" they groan as we turn our faces toward the rising sun in the east. They run toward the shaded portions of the sidewalk, seeking shelter in the shadows made by the oak and maple trees growing along our street.

If you've ever been without a hat or sunglasses on a bright, hot summer day, you know the relief you get from finding some shade, whether under a tree or a patio umbrella or the narrow awning of a building. That little bit of cool, dark shadow in which to hide from the scorching sun becomes a shelter and a refuge from the oppressive midday heat.

That's the picture the psalmist gives us in the first two verses of Psalm 91—a comforting picture of our almighty God as a shelter, a picture of our Lord in whose shadow is a place of refuge and safety from the dangers of this broken and merciless world. You can almost imagine the sigh of relief that comes at the end of verse 2: "my God, in whom I trust." *Aaahhh* . . .

That's what we need, isn't it? Even when we don't face the physical dangers described by the psalmist in later verses—the snare of the fowler, arrows, or pestilence—we still long for a secure dwelling place. We want a place of refuge where we can hide and find rest when the demands of work and family and friends and all of those interconnected roles and responsibilities become overwhelming. We long for a place of mercy in which we can be forgiven and encouraged when we reveal our sins and shortcomings. We hope for a place of peace and contentment that cannot be shaken by the challenges and frustrations we face each day—whatever form those challenges and frustrations take, be they piles of laundry, papers to grade, bills to pay, or medical procedures to endure.

The good news is that because God Himself is our dwelling place, we can live each day content in our current circumstances and hopeful for whatever future God has planned for us. We can trust in the One who "richly and daily provides me with all that I need to support this body and life" (Small Catechism, First Article). And just as we can trust our Creator's provision, we can trust our Savior's presence. Jesus, our Savior, who loved us so much He conquered death and the grave, now dwells in us by the Holy Spirit given in Baptism, bringing us forgiveness of sins, life, and salvation. We are never alone, never in want of a comforter or helper. And we dwell together, resting peacefully in the cool shadow of our Lord's mighty fortress. *Aaahhh* . . .

> *Praise to the Lord, who has fearfully, wondrously, made you,*
> *Health has bestowed and, when heedlessly falling, has stayed you.*
> *What need or grief*
> *Ever has failed of relief?*
> *Wings of His mercy did shade you.* (LSB 790:3)

Right Where You Are

Picture this. You have a storm raging. Physically, spiritually, financially—take your pick. Where do you seek shelter?

In our storms, we often fret, worry, and try to fix it ourselves. We look to a trusted friend for advice or to the world via social media or the internet for answers. We get so caught up in the anxiety of the situation that we don't see the light at the end of the tunnel; we throw up our hands, fall to our knees, and give up. We cry out a desperate prayer to God as a last resort, wondering if He is even listening.

He is. Not only is He listening but He has also been ever so patiently waiting for you to seek Him. He has some promises for you in your storm:

* He *is* the light at the end of the tunnel (JOHN 8:12).

* He *is* our most trusted, reliable Friend (JOHN 15:13).

* He *is* the way, the truth, and the life (JOHN 14:6).

* He will *never* leave you nor forsake you (HEBREWS 13:5).

Jesus meets you right where you are and offers to shield you with His omnipresence (one of His many attributes). He fully knows you, fully loves you, and offers *you*, His child, His peace that surpasses all understanding (Philippians 4:7). You see, He is in control of the storm that seems so out of control to you. With the power of His Word, He can calm the storm if He so chooses. Or He can shelter you as it rages. He can allow the storm to draw you back into Him, into His presence, where you have always belonged. You see, God has goals too. He delights in you and wants you to lean on Him. God provides all we need in this earthly life. He gives us our daily bread.

Psalm 91:1–2 says, "He who dwells in the shelter of the Most High will abide in the shadow of the Almighty. I will say to the LORD, 'My refuge and my fortress, my God in whom I trust.'"

When God is your shelter, you are safe from the storm. When you abide in the shadow of the Almighty, you are in the presence of God—the sweet spot where heaven meets earth. When you say to the Lord, "My refuge and my fortress, my God, in whom I trust," God's blessings freely flow without hindrance. He loves you so much that even in our sinful, imperfect, weather-beaten state, He provides the ultimate and eternal shelter in salvation through His Son (Romans 5:8).

We find God and experience Him in many ways—through the hearing and reading of His Word, communing with others in the Lord's Supper, Baptism, and being physically present in church with other like-minded believers. We experience His presence when we learn and practice to "be still, and know that [He is] God" (Psalm 46:10).

God will be with you always, to the very end of the age (Matthew 28:20). And He never breaks His promises!

God Always Has Room

Years ago, while driving through South Dakota on our way from Wisconsin to Montana, my husband and I stopped for dinner in the city of Mitchell. After eating, we discussed whether we should find a hotel for the night or drive a little further. Since it was still early evening and we had many more miles to our ultimate destination, we decided to travel on. But when we finally decided to pull over for the night, we couldn't find a hotel room *anywhere*.

We ended up stopping at a rest area and sleeping for a few hours before driving on. We repeated the process whenever we could no longer keep our eyes open. Although we made it through that very long night, we would have much preferred a soft bed and a roof over our heads. Without proper shelter, we felt unprotected, exposed.

Psalm 91:1–2 tells us that in our journey through life, we can always have proper shelter—the shelter of the Most High God! I love the imagery of this passage. The words the psalmist chooses paint a beautiful picture of the dwelling place of God. Let's take a closer look at some of those words, starting with the verbs.

The Hebrew word *yashab* translated as *dwell* means "to remain, sit, abide." The rest stops in South Dakota had signs that warned us, "Vehicles are not permitted to park longer than two hours." We couldn't stay long-term. We needed to move on. But God doesn't move on from us. He welcomes us to abide with Him. We can dwell with Him. We can remain in His grace forever.

In the next phrase, the word *abide* means "to lodge or spend the night." God will never put up a "No Vacancy" sign. Whenever we find ourselves in a gloomy season of life, we don't have to go through the nights alone. God provides a place for us to rest and abide.

And where can we dwell? Where can we abide? In the shelter of the Most High. In Hebrew, the noun translated to *shelter* can mean a covering—like a roof that protects us from rain and snow—but it can also mean a secret hiding place. When my husband and I slept in our car that night in South Dakota, we felt exposed. Although the roof of the car protected us from the elements, we knew potential robbers could see us through the windows. But when we stay in the shelter of the Most High God, He shields us from our spiritual enemies. We can also "abide in the shadow of the Almighty" (v. 1). The word *shadow* might conjure up images of scary, dark alleys. But think instead of seeing the shadow or shade of a giant maple tree right after you've finished a two-mile walk in the hot sun. God invites us to come close enough to sit in His shadow, to be refreshed in the shade and covering of His love.

When we feel threatened and chased by the world, we have a place to go. When it seems we are driving through darkness with no end in sight, we have a spot to spend the night. Because of Jesus Christ's work on the cross, God's protecting arms continually invite us close. He will never put up the "No Vacancy" sign on the shelter of His love.

He Feared Nothing

In a faint voice, I heard, "Sister, sing to me, please." These were the last words spoken to me by a brother from my church before he passed away from COVID-19 in November 2020. What a faithful and fearless servant of God. After suffering for a couple of weeks in the hospital, my friend knew in his heart that he was not returning to his home.

During a phone conversation one evening, he asked me to join him in praising our God in song, which brought him peace. In such a dark moment in his life, he feared nothing. He wasn't like much of the world, living in fear and doubt. The psalmist writes, "You will not fear the terror of the night, nor the arrow that flies by day, nor the pestilence that stalks in darkness, nor the destruction that wastes at noonday" (vv. 5–6).

During the pandemic, fear has paralyzed our entire world, and we have faced challenges that have caused stress and anxiety. Church doors closed, we practiced social distancing, and hospitals were at capacity, treating people with an illness we knew little about. Not to mention the overwhelming number of unexpected deaths. How do we teach our children to not fear? How do we respond to "Where is God?" when everything around us is crumbling before our eyes? How do we hold fast to the promises of God amid chaos?

As believers, our response to fear is and always will be to have a close relationship with the Lord. As the psalmist puts it, "He who dwells in the shelter of the Most High will abide in the shadow of the Almighty" (v. 1).

Because of my friend's relationship with Jesus, the peace that surpasses all understanding overflowed his life to the very end.

I believe that this very shelter (Jesus) gave him comfort and love, and prompted him to turn all his fears into faith. He trusted the Lord with the lives of those he would be leaving behind. "I will say to the LORD, 'My refuge and my fortress, my God, in whom I trust'" (v. 2).

Fear can keep us from enjoying the present, regardless of what may be taking place around us. But when God raised Jesus from the dead (Romans 8:11), He freed us from the fear of death and all the fears that go with it. "Under His wings you will find refuge" (v. 4). When we have faith in Jesus Christ as our Redeemer and Savior, we can face tomorrow without fear.

Prayer: Lord, nothing fills me more than being with You. In the storm, You keep me calm because Your faithfulness to me is constant. You restore my soul repeatedly, and Your love surrounds me. You are always faithful; when I speak, You hear my cry. I can trust in You because You have held me, time and time again. It's because of Your Word that I will not give up. Lord, I will always trust in You.

Lord, thank You that I can dwell in Your shelter and rest in Your shadow. Thank You for raising Jesus from the dead and freeing me from all my sins. For You are my refuge and my fortress and in You, my Lord, I can always trust. In Jesus' name I pray. Amen.

Lessons from Psalm 91:1–2 and the Closet Floor

My husband and I live near the Gulf Coast with our four kids. We love living so close to the water. We don't love the deadly hurricanes that strike almost every year between June and November. These massive storms bring triple-digit wind gusts and several feet of water to our neighborhoods.

When there's a storm in the Gulf, our family performs the same frantic ritual to protect our house and ourselves. We barricade the windows. We elevate furniture and appliances so they're above the storm surge. We move our cars to higher ground. When we've done what we can—and the wind and rain start—our family hunkers down.

It's strange to admit, but the very real threat of wind and rain feels almost quaint in our modern world. Nowadays, I'm trying to protect my family from an invisible virus and the constant mixture of dread and anxiety in the air and on the news.

Storms, though? They're loud and scary, but we're inside and safe. We are in our dwelling place, together, praying and remembering how Jesus powerfully calmed a similar storm (Mark 4:35–41).

In 2017, when Hurricane Harvey blew ashore, we huddled together in a little closet and hid from the many tornadoes. That night of huddling together in a stuffy, cluttered closet has weirdly become a treasured memory for our kids. They reminisce about listening to the constant tornado alerts as we held our breath and one another. They remember how we all got the giggles after so many hours of being cooped up inside, listening to the gusting wind and rain. They talk about how they felt so secure with our prayers, family, and safe place.

To be clear, we do not relish hurricanes, and we pray constantly for them to stay away. Yet there is something so secure about huddling together with your family in a place you trust is safe.

You, dear sister in Christ, know exactly what I mean because you have been there. Maybe you haven't hunkered down in a stuffy, crowded closet to protect your family, but you have done something better.

You have experienced the secure dwelling place of our almighty God (Psalm 91:1–2) through your adoption as His daughter. You've hunkered down with your family and prayed for God to spare you from the storms of grief, pride, hatred, sickness, anger, and sin. You have experienced the complete peace of God's security. You have trusted His strength and protection, even as you've realized your weakness as a mom, daughter, sister, aunt, or grandmother.

What have you experienced as those storms of fear raged around you? Gratitude that you worship a powerful God? Closeness to your Savior, Jesus, who was powerful enough to stop a storm and humble enough to die for our sins? Assurance through the Holy Spirit that you will be taken care of for eternity?

When you're afraid of your weaknesses and ability to protect your family, look to the names for God in Psalm 91:1–2. Our God is "shelter," "shadow," "refuge," and "fortress."

These names remind you that there is a place so safe that you can truly rest in the comfort of God's promises to hold you and your family close. Even when God's plans are not ours, He always loves us and always takes perfect care of us.

Trust in that security, dear friend. Know your Father is protecting you from the storms that could attack your family. Hold tight to the promise of eternal life with Him.

He is your dwelling place.

The Safe Place

S he stood in the middle of the resource center, looking like a deer caught in headlights, frozen in place. She seemed not to know where to look, which agency to approach first. Would danger strike again? Would she be safe here? Would there be someone to rescue her?

I met Susan that day. She and her sister had come to the Red Cross Resource Center to find help after a tornado had blown their mobile home off the map. And not only theirs, but their father's and a brother's mobile homes had disappeared as well. (When the tornado sirens had gone off, this family of eleven had taken shelter at the local Walmart.) Susan needed to find an abiding place that day—and for many days to come.

How often do we find ourselves in a similar situation following the death of a loved one or when an alienation springs up unexpectedly with a friend or family member; when a promise is broken or an expected job offer falls through; when we feel isolated because of illness or a contagious disease; when the anticipated phone call doesn't come; when the anguish of our own sin threatens to keep us in its dreadful grasp; when local or world news becomes overwhelming?

Psalm 91:1 uses two of my favorite words: *dwells* and *abide*. Both give a sense of peace, safety, comfort, and shelter from dangers. That's what God longs for us, His own dear children, to know: He is our dwelling place. He is our refuge. He is our abode.

One of my granddaughters once crawled to me as I worked at my desk. I picked her up and held her close as I finished some work at my computer. When I glanced down at her just a few minutes later, she had closed her eyes and was sound asleep.

She had found a dwelling place, a place of abiding. She had no fear. She had confidently come to me and fallen asleep in my arms.

There are times in the buffeting of life when I go to my heavenly Father for comfort. At those times, I feel as if I am crawling into my Father's lap for safekeeping. And He tenderly puts His arms around me to hold me close, to give me refuge and an abiding place. For the sake of Jesus' suffering and death, He assures me of His forgiveness.

Though dangers swirl around us, though life seems to catch us in a whirlpool of despair, though the shame and guilt of our own sin push us to the brink of hopelessness, we can trust God. We can know that He is, indeed, our refuge; we are safe in His loving arms; and He gives comfort, forgiveness in Jesus, safety and protection, reconciliation, and love. He promised. And God always keeps His promises.

Prayer: Dear heavenly Father, You are my abiding place where I can dwell in safety and security. You give me comfort and peace, a refuge from all that can overwhelm me. Thank You, Father, thank You. In Jesus' name I pray. Amen.

Pouring It All Out

Not long ago, I met myself for the first time. Granted, I have always been me. I just have not taken time to discover what that meant. For many years, I was too busy trying to become the woman others expected—or at least the woman I thought they expected.

Resting in the shelter of the Most High has taught me to appreciate the woman God created me to be and to take time to get comfortable with myself. As I rest secure in the waters of my Baptism, washed clean and made new, I can more confidently live out the calling God has given me. I am no longer sitting on my heels and waiting until I have perfected my portfolio. Instead, I am taking stock of the tools God has placed in my hands for this season and putting them to good use.

In Matthew 26:6–13, we hear about another woman who took the valuable resources she had and poured them out for her Lord. This woman, led by the Holy Spirit, perhaps knew that Jesus was about to sacrifice all for His people. She entered the house where Jesus was dining and poured a lavishly expensive perfume from an alabaster flask over Jesus' head.

The disciples and guests were critical of the woman. *What a waste! Why not sell the perfume and give the proceeds to the poor?* But she wasn't performing for them. This was an act of worship. She was demonstrating her gratitude for the great price Jesus was about to pay for His people. She was acknowledging Him as the King of kings. Jesus defended her action as a "beautiful thing" (v. 10) and declared, "Wherever this gospel is proclaimed in the whole world, what she has done will also be told in memory of her" (v. 13).

What is your alabaster jar? What treasures has the Lord given you today to pour out to Him in worship? Embrace the woman God has created you uniquely to be. Use the sphere of influence you have at this minute to help spread the Gospel story. As you rest in His presence, let Him fill you with His Spirit. Then be brave enough to pour everything out upon the King of kings. In His hands, He can use it to do immeasurably more than we can even imagine.

Anxious to Abide

S *helter, shadow, refuge, fortress.* These words in Psalm 91:1–2 are thick with protection, solidly resonating with offered rest and restoration. *Dwell* and *abide* are verbs of invitation, beckoning us in to come and stay awhile, still and secure in a place of safety. These times of God-gifted rest are usually marked by a pairing of solitude and silence, whether deep in nature or perhaps a pane of glass away. A rainy Sunday afternoon on a great old front porch. A prayerful walk through the park under a soaring cathedral ceiling of tree branches. Curled up on the sofa, the quiet like a quilt, soft and timeless and achingly comforting.

Dear sister, I don't know what is true for you in your season of life, but for me, as I relive such times in memory, my vision blurs with longing. It is busy, this life—full of worthy vocational demands—ones that give purpose and joy, discipline and direction, ones that serve neighbor and honor relationships.

How good it is to have a God worth longing for.

How hard it is to find the space to meet Him well.

Why is it hard? It seems simple enough—follow the directions as penned by the psalmist. Dwell, abide, stay in the shadow. Navigate through the ups and downs and crevices of my calendar to find the open spaces that would be refuge. Yet it seems the harder I work at finding rest, the more it slips away and the more disheartened I become.

So I make a new plan: I will simply abide better! Here I will scratch out the perimeters of Nothing Else on my calendar page. There I will honor the temple that is my Creator-given body. Especially there, on Sunday morning, I will establish a fortress of focus, heaven-bent to concentrate on who He is and what He does and what He means to me.

But again, I fail to hold the lines. My vocations, the joys and demands of them, spill over the boundaries of my calendar spaces, siphon away my body's energy, and crowd out any margin in my life. These good gifts are also heavy responsibilities, yet at times they compete for brain space, and it seems I catch only a fraction of even the best sermon.

Pressed for time and pressed for joy, I read the psalmist's words and feel like crying out for the wanting of their truth in my life: Where is my refuge, O Lord? Jesus withdrew to His mountains and gardens. Even Elijah got not one but two full nights of sleep and breakfast in bed! In these moments, I know to approach the seat of mercy. I go, though not with the smooth grace of a seasoned believer but all the emotional instability of a preschooler who has missed a week's worth of naps. I am tired, and I know it, and I need my Daddy. Now.

The beautiful thing is, my heavenly Father sits with me through my tears until they are spent. Then, just as beautifully, He helps me see that the foundations of my fortress have slipped. First, He perfectly and wisely wields the level of Law to show that I have not truly grasped how off-balance things have become. Here I have said yes to too much, there is the right thing but in the wrong place. In this thorough inspection of the state of my soul, the Holy Spirit in grace stays with me as I acknowledge and repent. This chipping and stripping away is uncomfortable but also deeply relieving. As I reevaluate, my soul feels clean, ready to try again. But before I can take up the effort, the Lord makes a move that takes my breath away; He flips the gravity of my fortress completely.

He says to me, "Beloved, why are you anxious for abiding? I AM already here. You are grounded in Me. I AM in, with, and under your every waking moment. I, who do not sleep, guard the shadowed hours of your rest, however few they may seem. It is true—you alone are not sufficient for your day. Dear daughter, I have a better truth: you are never alone. Remember the cross; I was forsaken in your place. I endured complete absence so that you will always have My full presence. I am with you to the end."

Braced with this comforting truth, I recognize that retreating from the world for a time is a good and healthy spiritual discipline. With Spirit-led discernment, I can create space for those encounters. Yet even in the valleys between the mountaintops, where the chaos of this world batters against my heart, I can tuck my soul under His promises and remember that the Lord God dwells in me. He overshadows my steps even as He directs them. God, my refuge, chooses to tabernacle in my very body, reinforcing my days with the strength of His love and establishing my future on the firm footing of His truth.

Prayer: Lord God, You are our cornerstone. We confess that at times we try to stake our security to our own best-laid plans, yet all the while You beckon us to build our hope on You alone. When it feels like the walls are closing in, help us remember the One who broke through the walls of the tomb to win life for us. When we are at the end of our patience, the end of our endurance, the end of our sanity, anchor us to You and imbed the assurance of Your presence deeper within us. Help us live out our days in joyful, active acknowledgment of Your truth, that You are with us to the very end of this age, and on to the limitless joys of the next. Amen.

Who trusts in God

A strong abode

In heav'n and earth possesses;

Who looks in love

To Christ above,

No fear that heart oppresses.

In You alone,

Dear Lord, we own

Sweet hope and consolation,

Our shield from foes,

Our balm for woes,

Our great and sure salvation.

(LSB 714:1)

Yoga Pants and Ponytails

O ne of my all-time favorite things to do when I get home is to put my hair up in a ponytail, change into my comfies, and sit back on the couch. After a long day, I look forward to unwinding in the comfort of my own home. My cares, worries, and stresses seem to melt away when my yoga pants are on and my ponytail is up.

There's something about coming home, isn't there? After all, home is where we let our guard down, live authentically, and seek rest from the wearied world. It's the place that meets our unpainted faces and disheveled hair with hospitality and warmth. Yet as I reflected upon my unfeigned delight in coming home after a long day, I realized that for many recently, our homes have transitioned into offices, classrooms, overflows for the unemployed, and places of isolation and quarantine. Countless numbers watched the rest, refuge, and relaxation drain from their homes right before their eyes. What once was an oasis and safe haven transformed into a cesspool of negativity, uncertainty, and anxiety.

The saying "home is where the heart is" got me thinking about where my heart has resided lately. Have I been living in the divisive nature of our world? Have I dwelt in fear and paranoia? Have I rested in discouragement and flirted with hopelessness? Have I built a shelter of bitterness and apathy?

Psalm 91:1–2 says, "He who dwells in the shelter of the Most High will abide in the shadow of the Almighty. I will say to the LORD, 'My refuge and my fortress, my God, in whom I trust.'"

God zealously invites our hearts to take up residency with Him! He's not looking for us to check in on Sundays for a guest visit. Instead, He eagerly anticipates our permanent stay with Him! As the King of hospitality,

* ❦ He desires to prepare a table for us. (PSALM 23:5);

* ❦ He provides a place for us to lie down, rest, and dwell in safety (PSALM 4:8);

* ❦ He tells us to come to Him with our worries and burdens (MATTHEW 11:28);

* ❦ He promises to supply all our needs (PHILIPPIANS 4:19);

* ❦ His listening skills are paramount because His ears are attentive to our prayers (1 PETER 3:12); and

* ❦ He renews the strength of those who hope in Him (ISAIAH 40:31).

We can come to Him in yoga pants, without makeup, and with crumply hair. He isn't waiting for us to clean ourselves up. He is yearning for us to return to Him (Isaiah 44:22) so He can do the cleaning! Jesus' arms are where we unabashedly run to let our guards down, live authentically, and seek spiritual rest from a sinful world. He is waiting eagerly for your arrival and permanent stay.

Have you intentionally taken time to rest in the shelter of our loving Father? In what ways can you seek refuge in Him this week?

Prayer: Dear God, we praise You for who You are. You are our good, good Father. You are our Savior, Redeemer, and Comforter. You are our Intercessor, Teacher, and Guide. Thank You for being our resting place and home base. Thank You for the safety, protection, and refreshment You give to our hearts. Forgive us when our hearts take refuge in worldly things and draw us into a deeper relationship with You. In Jesus' name we pray. Amen.

Personal Reflection

For He will deliver you from the snare of
   the fowler

   and from the deadly pestilence.

He will cover you with His pinions,

   and under His wings you will find refuge;

   His faithfulness is a shield and buckler.

You will not fear the terror of the night,

   nor the arrow that flies by day,

nor the pestilence that stalks in darkness,

   nor the destruction that wastes at noonday.

A thousand may fall at your side,

   ten thousand at your right hand,

   but it will not come near you.

You will only look with your eyes

   and see the recompense of the wicked.

PART 2

Psalm 91:3–8

....

AUTHORS

....

Alli Bauck

Terri Bentley

Amy Bird

Elizabeth Bruick

Faith Doerr

Margo Heath-Dupre

Wendysue Fluegge

Angie Goeke

Heidi Goehmann

Hannah Hansen

Lindsay Hausch

Sarah Holtan

Haleh Kersten

Pat Maier

Cassie Moore

Raquel A. Rojas

Heather Ruesch

Hannah van Dellen

By Night as by Day

My infant son and I are playing upstairs. He turns to look up at me; five little teeth peek through his gummy grin. And then he starts speed-crawling toward the stairs. His hand outstretched, he teeters above the top step—

I wake with a jolt, heart pounding, surrounded by the peaceful darkness of my bedroom. A nightlight glows in the empty hallway. My son is safely asleep in his crib.

I struggle daily to protect my children. Whether from physical harm or hidden dangers, I often feel unable to shield their young lives from earthly threats. Even in my dreams, I am taunted by the reality that I am helpless!

Psalm 91:3–8 emphasizes God's omnipotence over the perils of this life. Despite "snare[s]," "pestilence," "terror[s]," "arrow[s]," and "destruction," the Almighty will always "deliver," "cover," "shield," and faithfully protect His children from bodily harm. As believers on this side of the cross, we not only have the assurance that God *can* preserve our daily lives from difficulties but we also *know* that He desires our souls to be saved. By sending His only Son, Jesus, as a sacrifice, God has provided an eternal refuge for us in the new creation. While we wait for Christ's return, we have the grace of Holy Baptism, the promises of Scripture, and the forgiveness of sins through the Sacrament of Holy Communion.

As much as I wish my children could be exempt from suffering, I do not have to live in fear of the evils in this world. When my head, heart, and hands fail to keep my family safe, I can rest in the grace God gives and entrust my life—and theirs—to His protective safety. Like the psalmist, we need to place our faith in God, not in ourselves. Instead of feeling helpless and hopeless, we need to seek the Lord's refuge, abiding in Him when fearful times arise. He created us, and He will sustain us—in this earthly life and the life of the world to come.

Often when I am feeling discouraged in my faith walk, the Spirit speaks peace into my anxious heart. The words come from friends, family, Scripture, or from a hymn like "Christ Be My Leader" (*LSB* 861), which points to the Word Incarnate. (I commend stanzas 1 and 3 for your personal meditation, or seek solace in another hymn that brings peace to your soul.)

Will you take a minute to personalize the paraphrased verses below? Let this be a prayer and a promise. Our heavenly Father has delivered us from sin and death, He covers and shields us with His love and provision, and He will faithfully continue to hold us by night as by day. The challenges we face are temporary.

God will deliver [your name] from [hidden dangers that threaten you physically]. He will cover you, and you will find refuge; His faithfulness is a shield and protection. You will not fear the [emotional fear] nor [wars/battles] nor [daily threats to the Christian life]. Multitudes may fall around you, but evil will not come near you, [your name]. You will look with your own eyes and witness the punishment of those who rebel against God.

When We Collide with Disaster

I was driving home from sitting with my daughter during her weekly chemo treatment. Breast cancer had invaded our lives. Now chemotherapy, radiation, and surgery lay ahead.

The hour-long drive on familiar mountainous Idaho roads helped calm my anxiety over hospital settings and a suffering daughter. There was no need for a scenic drive sign to announce views that grace calendars and computer wallpaper—the Payette River and its rapids carve steep valleys into the mountains to form a stunningly beautiful scene. And the beautiful drive was the way back to my cabin retreat.

Then *bam!* A fully grown bald eagle smashed into my face, stopped only by my car's windshield. I jumped. My heart pounded, and I pulled over, shaking. The eagle, with its six-foot wingspan, hovered for a moment then was gone. Did it crack the windshield? I had been going at least fifty miles per hour.

I ventured out to discover only a small scratch on the glass. What about the bird? I walked along the road, looking in the ditches for the majestic creature. There was no sign of him. Isn't there a fine for killing an endangered species? What should I do?

As I stood there, trying to calm my racing heart and catch my breath, I heard a screech. Above me, on a rock outcropping, perched the eagle. He was watching me. He had been fishing the river and glided up over the road when we crossed paths. The collision had to have left him dazed and hurting.

What happens when we collide with disaster out of the blue?

❋ A mother suffers a stroke that results in her death.

❋ A daughter is stricken with breast cancer.

❋ Another daughter contracts COVID-19.

❋ I receive news of a mass in my uterus.

Does the impact of life's crashes leave me lying in a ditch? Or do I allow God to lift me above the turmoil?

> *For He will deliver you from the snare of the fowler*
> *and from the deadly pestilence.*
> *He will cover you with His pinions,*
> *and under His wings you will find refuge;*
> *His faithfulness is a shield and buckler.* (Psalm 91:3–4)

Bad news leaves me dazed, bent, and battered, but God is the refuge I need. His Word and Sacraments are wings that raise me above troubled times so I can look at the situation from a solid perspective. I tremble and cry. But the faithful Lord shields me and girds me for what lies ahead.

The eagle flew on to fish another day; the Lord equips us to fish another day too. The kingdom of heaven is like a net that is thrown into the sea and gathers fish of every kind (see Matthew 13:47). God draws us to Himself in the safety net of His Gospel in every collision, fright, threat, and trouble. Almighty God draws us to Himself and delivers us from every snare that sin and the evil one sends to entrap us. He offers refuge under the outstretched arms of His Son, our Savior, and covers us with compassion, love, and hope in His promise of heaven.

And He never lets me down!

Under His Wings

I've watched plenty of cat videos online when I've needed a good laugh or the soothing comfort of a purr. But I hadn't searched for a hen protecting her chicks until preparing to write this devotion. Complete transparency: the videos brought me to tears.

In one video, the hen puffs up her chest, spreads her wings wide, and approaches the threat head-on—putting herself between the danger and her children. In another, little chicks nestle together under mom's coverage, their heads popping out every once in a while to look around.

Why did these images bring me to tears? Because I wanted to be the chick in that moment, protected on all sides and able to hide, buffered from threat under the protection of mom's wing. The chicks seemed to wait patiently, knowing they were safe in mom's refuge.

One summer weekend when I was eight years old, my family went to a nearby lake. It wasn't uncommon for us to go fishing. But on this day, we were going tubing.

I'd never been before, and when it was my turn to go, I modestly knelt in the tube, life vest strapped around my chest, and held on as the boat picked up speed. I'm sure everything was relatively gentle and slow, but to me, it was so exhilarating—both fun and scary. It didn't take long for a small wave to throw me off, and into the water. In my alarm, I opened my eyes underwater and saw blurry white shapes moving around and a glistening green surrounding me. I panicked. As if forgetting I was wearing a life vest (and knew how to swim), I thought I was drowning.

I surfaced immediately, flailed my arms as I bobbed up and down in the wake, and screamed.

As soon as my mom heard my cry, she dove from the boat into the water. She swam out and pulled me into her arms. Mom held me, made sure I wasn't hurt, and brought me back to the boat. Once on the boat, she wrapped a towel around my shoulders and reassured me that I was safe. Then I noticed her heel bleeding . . . a lot. She'd cut her foot when she jumped from the boat, a mom-instinct move that would land her on crutches with stitches for six weeks.

This memory reminds me of a mother hen protecting her chicks. It also brings me to the image of God described in Psalm 91 as a bird covering His little ones from any trap or threat:

> *For He will deliver you from the snare of the fowler*
> *and from the deadly pestilence.*
> *He will cover you with His pinions,*
> *and under His wings you will find refuge;*
> *His faithfulness is a shield and buckler.* (PSALM 91:3–4)

Looking back on this story of younger me, I know I was in no real danger. No creature in the water could harm me. And even if my swim lessons would have failed me, my life jacket wouldn't. Furthermore, my mom was watching and ready to assist at any moment.

As children of God, we know nothing can take us from Christ. And even if our knowledge of Scripture or wisdom in the Spirit fails us, our Baptism holds us secure. Being buried with Christ and raised to new life in Him, we have the promise that no power can stand against us. Still, at the sound of our cries, God doesn't leave us in our struggle or despair. He sends Himself to us again and again, fully and personally in the body and blood of Christ. At the Table, we're reminded of God's love for us—that Christ is with us and in us.

Though the devil might strike the heel of Christ's foot, his head has been crushed. There is no snare, terror, or deadly pestilence that Jesus cannot protect us from. Under His wings, we find refuge.

Though devils all the world should fill,
All eager to devour us,
We tremble not, we fear no ill;
They shall not overpow'r us.
This world's prince may still
Scowl fierce as he will,
He can harm us none.
He's judged; the deed is done;
One little word can fell him. (LSB 656:3)

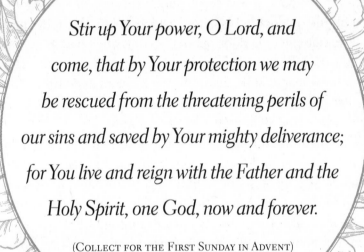

Stir up Your power, O Lord, and come, that by Your protection we may be rescued from the threatening perils of our sins and saved by Your mighty deliverance; for You live and reign with the Father and the Holy Spirit, one God, now and forever.

(Collect for the First Sunday in Advent)

Afraid of the Dark

I grew up in a suburban area with streetlights and porch lights on many neighboring houses. Nights there were never truly dark. After I got married, my husband and I lived outside the city, distanced from other houses and without streetlights. It wasn't just dark, it was eerily dark, especially if we forgot to turn on the outdoor lights before we left home. We didn't have an automatic garage door opener, so one of us had to get out of the car, unlock the garage door, and open it manually. Had I ever been scared of the dark? Not until I had to do this. What was I scared of? Whatever my imagination said was lurking in the shadows and stalking me in the darkness.

One night when I was by myself, as I hurriedly unlocked the door and was about to walk into the garage, I glanced over my shoulder. The moon shone brightly that night, and it was beautiful. In my fear, I had missed the beauty. In my fear, I had missed the peace that comes with such a calming sight. I didn't allow room for anything else other than what I was scared of. I have a lot of fears, but when I remember that night, no matter what kind of fear it is, I remind myself to turn and see God's presence all around, to appreciate the beauty and peace He provides.

Sometimes our fears, sins, and the ways we fall short get the best of us. We can't function and don't know what to do or where to turn. But God covers us, and we can find refuge in Him. Once we give up our spirit, we'll know the freedom we have in Christ.

That freedom allows us to dwell in His deliverance and His complete faithfulness to us—a deliverance and faithfulness we don't want to live without. God is with us. He is for us. He is all powerful and mightier than we give Him credit for. He is worthy of our trust. If He can feed thousands with five loaves and two fish, He can provide for us too.

One of the things I love about our God is that He is in the big things *and* the little things. He cares for His people—for you and me. The more we trust Him and see Him move and work in our lives and the lives of those around us, the more He becomes not just God in heaven but God in our hearts, dwelling within us as we received in our Baptism. We can face each new day adventurously and expectantly, trusting that God knows us better than we do.

We will not "fear the terror of the night . . . nor the pestilence . . . nor the destruction" (Psalm 91:5–6). He is with you in the darkness. He will always deliver you and cover you with His mercy and love.

Prayer: What fears do you have? Pray that God would deliver you from them and renew your confidence in His power and provision.

Our Ultimate Deliverer

One day last summer, my husband, Preston, was doing yard work. He came inside and said, "You have to see this." I rose from playing on the floor with our son, Ezekiel, and we all went outside. *What on earth did he want us to see?* In the backyard was an ice cream bucket flipped over to cover something. Preston gently lifted the bucket to reveal a baby bunny.

Instead of springing to life and running away, this bunny just laid there. As we stepped closer, we could see its stomach barely moving. Its fur was wet and bloodied, and it looked like it had been attacked by another animal. It was hanging onto life by a thread.

"Should we wipe the dirt and leaves off it?" my husband asked.

I thought we should, so I ran into the house for a towel. Slowly and carefully, Preston wiped the bunny dry. We laid the bunny in the sun, hoping the warmth of the rays would help revive it. After a couple of minutes, we decided to call our local animal control to have them take it to a refuge.

While we waited for animal control, I realized I was nervous for the bunny. There are many hawks in our neighborhood. *What if a hawk comes and tries to snatch it?* I scanned the trees, ready to hover over the bunny and shoo a predator away.

At this moment, I thought about our relationship with God. How often are we like this helpless bunny? We get lost in the weeds and attacked by the spiritual predators of this world. We find ourselves hanging on by a thread, feeling like we can't come out of it. There is no end in sight.

Then God comes beside us and reminds us that we are washed clean by the waters of our Baptism. Satan wants us to feel trapped in our sin, bogged down by the worries of this world, and broken and worried about hawks coming for us, just like that small bunny. Yet God will not let us be crippled by sin. He restores us and provides protection.

When we have those moments of anxiousness—*I don't know if I can do this. I feel uncomfortable and uncertain*—the evil one tries to get us to stay there. He wants us to remain in those thoughts and that funk. In that state, we are not in the light of Christ. We are in the shadow of uncertainty and fear.

Yet even as we are entangled in Satan's talons, God unclenches Satan's hold on us and brings us under His wings. He sees the scars that have been left by Satan's grasp and heals us.

Sin can have a hold on us that causes us to feel hopelessly trapped. And in fact, we are. We cannot free ourselves from it. God gives us the ultimate deliverer in Christ Jesus. Our Savior defeated Satan once for all. Satan is no threat to us.

While we will still have thoughts of anxiety and despair on this side of heaven, Jesus is living proof that one day we will not. That bunny did nothing to get help from Preston, me, or the animal control officer. Yet it received help anyway. That's how God works for us. We do nothing to deserve the grace only He provides, yet He freely gives it despite our shortcomings, our anxious thoughts, and temptations. One day, we will not be dragged down by the trials of this world but will be lifted up by the grace of Christ Jesus.

Sometimes Our Own Worst Enemy

The world tells us to focus on how we feel about things instead of what we think or believe. This "natural" way of responding is how people expect us to understand what is real in the world. When asked about issues, we often hear others start by saying, "I feel." Our feelings affect decision-making, behaviors, and attitudes. Some feelings cause a distorted view of reality, blocking our sense of what is right and wrong and causing us to function at times as our own worst enemy. If we allow our emotions to guide our minds, we experience frustration, confusion, sleepless nights, days fraught with disappointment, and a sense of inadequacy and helplessness. Since this response puts the focus entirely on ourselves, we may start to doubt the Word of God.

We don't have to live this way! In John 6:63, Christ told His disciples, "It is the Spirit who gives life; the flesh is no help at all." His promise of the Holy Spirit (see John 14:16) comes to us when we are baptized. The indwelling of the Holy Spirit keeps us in the true faith. He is purposely and intimately fused within us, influencing our thoughts and emotions such as grief, love, kindness, grace, and, yes, anger (see Ephesians 4:29–32).

God designed us to experience feelings that cause an emotional response. It is a very personal way to connect to Him and one another. In other words, we feel because God Himself feels. God created us with feelings that are intended to be used in our lives according to His divine purpose. "For all who are led by the Spirit of God are sons of God" (Romans 8:14).

However, God has also given us the gift of free will—the ability to think and reason. Along with the help of the Holy Spirit, who ministers to us through the study of Scripture, we can discern life circumstances and no longer dwell on emotions and thoughts that distance us from God (see 1 John 1:5–10).

Having faith in Jesus does not exempt us from sinning, nor does it stop us from doubting God's Word. Even so, out of love for us, He offered Himself as a sacrifice to make amends for our sins through His work of eternal salvation. "And the peace of God, which surpasses all understanding, will guard your hearts and your minds in Christ Jesus" (Philippians 4:7). The Word of God has the power to change our lives!

With the help of the Holy Spirit, who intercedes for us in our daily prayer life and ministers to us in the study of God's Holy Word, we can focus our minds on the unchangeable character of God, be comforted by His promise, and rest in the certainty of His control over all circumstances.

Prayer: Thank You, heavenly Father, for giving me Your Holy Word and sending the Holy Spirit as a Comforter who constantly leads me to You and Your everlasting love.

Our Best Shot

For He will deliver you from the snare of the fowler
and from the deadly pestilence.
He will cover you with His pinions,
and under His wings you will find refuge;
His faithfulness is a shield and buckler. (PSALM 91:3–4)

We've all become better at hiding. We had a reason. A deadly pestilence swept through the world. Many fought illness and death. Extended families were separated. Sadness and fear invaded hearts. During quarantine, some welcomed more privacy and rest. Others had more quiet time than they wanted and enough Zooming for life. We locked down communities, closed churches, covered faces, washed hands, scrubbed surfaces, vaccinated bodies, kept our distance, and followed recommendations while praying for protection. We desired to be wise and longed to stay safe. "Vaccinations: Our Best Shot" became the slogan.

Yet the reality is no lockdown, mask, medication, cleaning product, or protective measure will save us. These things are helpful and certainly can be used by the Great Physician. However, the Scriptures remind us that the Lord protects, provides, delivers, and numbers our days.

He will deliver you from the snare. . . . *He* will
cover you . . . under *His* wings you will find refuge.
(PSALM 91:3–4, EMPHASIS ADDED)

Jesus is our Best Shot—and the only everlasting hope.

The "pinions" that cover us refer to the outermost parts of a wing that allow full flight capability. What a sweet picture of receiving God's whole wing. Rather than part of or most of, we get every millimeter, from tip to tip. Ultimate safety with maximum aviation! Sometimes we're lifted *on* those wings. Sometimes we're hidden *under* them.

"His faithfulness is a shield and buckler" (v. 4). A buckler is a small shield that is worn on the wrist and held firmly with a handle. It is used in personal defense. Our Father's faithfulness is a defense tool? Whoa! That means you and I can fight disease, doubt, and difficulty by holding up prayer, praise, and proclamation. We can attack the day of trouble while gushing the greatness and goodness of God.

The psalmist may have penned these verses after hiding from a powerful enemy who desired to kill him. As he hid, the psalmist may have recalled a story of unlikely defeat, that of David over the Philistine giant with the name of the Lord Almighty, a sling, and five stones. Victory came because the Lord was faithfully fighting.

How battle-ready are you? Grab that buckler. Take note of the past. Review the track record. Acknowledge every promise God fulfilled, every mistake He redeemed, every triumph He allowed, every issue He resolved, and every prayer He answered—just the way you'd asked. Tally them up to post, memorize, and declare. Compose a poem or song if you're like me:

I believe You are The God who holds me fast.

My strong Deliverer—so faithful in the past.

Rescue me. Come, restore.

Rescue me. I need You, Lord.

(FROM "RESCUE ME" INSPIRED BY PSALM 140 © 2020)

Rescue came at the cross when Jesus took the punishment of our sin upon Himself. The great deliverance of mankind happened at Calvary when love ran red and that perfect Lamb was sacrificed for all. Death was defeated when Christ broke from the tomb, rising on the third day. We are forgiven, guilt-free, and eternally secured through faith in Him. All else is secondary and shrinks in the shadow of the sovereign Spirit, who dwells within us, transforming us worriers into bold warriors.

So have no fear. Have faith. Take heart. Take shelter.

Take your Best Shot!

Lord, be our light when worldly darkness veils us;

Lord be our shield when earthly armor fails us;

And in the day when hell itself assails us,

Grant us Your peace, Lord:

Peace in our hearts, where sinful thoughts are raging,

Peace in Your church, our troubled souls assuaging,

Peace when the world its endless war is waging,

Peace in Your heaven. (LSB 659:3, 4)

The Problem with Good Intentions

A mother duck and her three little chicks had found their way to our backyard pool. It's hot on the Gulf Coast of Texas where we live, and this little family may have been looking for respite from the steaming pavement of the city. My four kids immediately took notice, gluing themselves to the sliding glass door. It wasn't long before my teenage girls were asking their smartphones: "Is chlorinated water harmful for birds?"

The internet answered with a yes. This mother duck had led her littles into a potentially deadly situation. More disconcerting than the chlorinated water is that most backyard pools don't have the sloping edges of a natural lake or pond to help flightless chicks find solid footing. The downy young can drown from exhaustion if they can't climb out.

This information was sufficient to spur my own downy boys into "savior mode." They ran to the garage, found plywood, and gingerly configured a ramp for the tiny trio. Their efforts, however, backfired. Momma Duck, keenly aware of the commotion, led her babies to every edge of the pool except the one with the convenient exit.

After forty-five minutes of shooing the duck family toward the ramp, we realized we were causing the little chicks to swim with exhaustive rigor as they followed their mother rim to rim like marbles in a pinball machine. We went back inside and patiently waited. Within minutes, Momma Duck located the roaming pool skimmer and guided her young to hop on the hose, using it as a step to get out of the pool to safety.

How often have someone else's best intentions actually caused us harm? fatigue? maybe some annoyance? A ramp was a fine idea, but it wasn't necessary; it was hurtful. Even with good intentions, we can hurt or be hurt by those we love. Spouses, an angry teenager, even a two-year-old can be ruthless toward those who love them the most.

It can be daunting when a loved one, with good intentions or not, wounds us. I know many women who have been devastatingly hurt by the sinful behavior of their husbands. Pornography, abandonment, physical and emotional abuse, for example, all stem from seeking one's own comforts and desires rather than serving a spouse out of love. When those intimately close to us land us in a wave of hurtful waters, it can be hard to process. It can be exhausting. Who do we lean on now? Who do we follow? The intensions of a spouse can be bifurcated, protecting self-interests even while also desiring to love perfectly. It's just what we humans do in our sinful nature. (I, too, struggle with this.) And it's confusing for those caught in the ripple effect.

Christ, on the other hand, is focused on us. He pursues our hearts with no concern for His own comforts. In taking His place on the cross, He gave all of Himself to save us. So even when those called to love and protect us fail, He is not distracted or divided in His intent. He remains faithful and steadfast and keenly aware of our situation. If you are hurting, let Him silence the commotion and lead you to the next safe step. Let Him guide you to lean on Him for solutions and saving. Perhaps that next step is forgiveness toward the one who hurt you. Maybe it's asking for outside help through a counselor. Maybe it's time spent waiting patiently on the Holy Spirit to reveal the way and His safe passage to solid ground. You are not alone. He is right beside you in the waters and has you safely under His wings.

Our Shield and Buckler

In modern Western culture, we tend to be *rah-rah!* kind of people:

"You can do it!"

"You've got this!"

"Keep your chin up!"

In the Christian Church, our rah-rah can come off even stronger because we *do* know we have everything we need in Christ. We *do* know that one day all will be well. We *do* know that there is a Healer in all things and of all things—our hearts, our souls, our minds, and our bodies.

Yet there are problems that rah-rah does not solve and times when rah-rah makes us feel unseen, unheard, and more distant from God rather than comforted and covered by the knowledge of all His healing and mercy. These problems may be wide and varied, but feeling distant from God and wanting to be seen and heard by those we love seems especially true when someone we know lives with mental health challenges.

In Psalm 91, we find raw truth about the problems of this world rather than rah-rah. The writer of the psalm lays out before the reader that which assails. Consider a few of the words from verses 3–6 from a mental health vantage point:

* Pestilence or plague—illness and disintegration, both physical and mental

* Darkness that stalks and creeps close to us—depression, hurt, shame, hopelessness, addiction, and suicide

* Destruction that wastes—family drama, heartache, injustice, and anxiety for ourselves, the children we love, and our world

In the psalm, we also find raw emotion rather than rah-rah. The psalmist uses words like *terror, fear, refuge,* and *faithfulness.* This psalm and the Book of Psalms as a whole look honestly at the dark and light sides of life and the complexity of holding them together during our time here on earth. We live in the now of our present challenges of brokenness. We also live in the promise of God's kindness and grace in the middle of it all—not only after it all, not when we've made it through it all. People around us—those we love who are struggling—need to know that there is an after. They need to know that there will be full restoration in Christ when He returns and that there is restoration in His arms now.

In Psalm 91, God does not rah-rah us. God covers us. God shields us. God shows us His love, directing our eyes again and again toward Jesus Christ on the cross for hope, the Word for meaning, and the community of God for help and support. God is with us. His Spirit lives in us. His faithfulness as a shield and buckler is a strong image. The shield is a large defense to cover the whole body. The buckler is a smaller defensive shield, covering only a specific area. The shield and buckler and God's wings of refuge are messages we can share with someone who is struggling, ourselves included. They are reminders that God sees us and is with us as we face both the massive problems in our lives and our smallest anxieties and concerns.

Take a moment now to go to God with those things and people in your life that need His refuge. Be assured that His grace in Christ Jesus is your deliverance every day, when we can be rah-rahed and when we can't.

Connection and Comfort

Hear my cry, O God,
listen to my prayer;
from the end of the earth I call to you
when my heart is faint. (PSALM 61:1–2)

I've felt helpless during many seasons in my life. I'm sure you've had those times too. There are times when you're waiting to see the light at the end of the tunnel (but all you see is the tunnel), times when nothing you do seems to matter, and times when God feels far away.

When the worries and stresses of life seem to consume your entire focus, it can feel like God isn't present. *Why would He let this happen to me? Why isn't He answering my prayers? When will this suffering end?*

For many of us, when we get busy and stressed, the first thing we cut is time with God. And so begins the vicious cycle—we don't prioritize our faith because God feels far away, but God only continues to feel far away from us the longer we go without seeking Him. And even if you are diligently praying and studying Scripture in your times of helplessness, God can still feel far away.

When I feel helpless and disconnected from God, I start to rely on tangible practices that connect me to Him. In church, I make the sign of the cross on my chest when the pastor begins the service with the Invocation. I intentionally touch my forehead, chest, and shoulders. During Communion, I remember that this is forgiveness made physical.

God also often uses ordinary people to speak His comfort into our lives. Pastors, church workers, spouses, parents, and friends can all be mouthpieces to share God's peace. Don't underestimate the importance of community in times of helplessness. Rely on those God has placed in your life to carry you through a hopeless season.

The devil and our own sinful nature can speak lies to us, telling us that God surely doesn't care about us, that we deserve this suffering, and that our prayers are not heard. But these are exactly that—lies.

God promises to love and care for His children. He may not provide for you in the way you hope, but He does provide. Through the preaching of His Word to the administration of the Sacraments, we can be reminded of His goodness and provision for us, no matter our circumstances.

In our Baptism, we were marked as Christ's own. He will never leave us or forsake us, no matter how messy life gets and no matter how hopeless we feel.

This Is No Fairy Tale

As we read in Psalm 91:3–8, the Bible doesn't paint a fairy tale world with flat, feel-good characters, but with raw and flawed people fighting an epic battle for survival.

One of my favorite heroes is David. David is vulnerable and brutally honest about life. In the psalms he wrote, David pours out his emotions to God without fear of looking like a wuss.

We do not know who wrote Psalm 91, but its author reveals a similar depth of humanity, fear and frailty, and the landscape of danger, bloodshed, and constant threat to life. In this psalm, we get a three-dimensional picture of how real and necessary faith in God is. It is in this desperate and dangerous picture that the psalmist paints God as deliverer, shield, and refuge.

Back to David: There's an awesome story in 1 Samuel 30 that offers a glimpse of how he lived out this reality, and I believe it serves as a great model for how we can apply it as we face our own life challenges.

The story begins with a devastating picture. David and his men have returned to their camp in Ziklag to discover that it has been raided and burned down by the Amalekites. To make matters worse, the Amalekites have taken all of their wives and children captive. In response, "David and the people who were with him raised their voices and wept until they had no more strength to weep" (v. 4).

Devastation, heartbreak, loss—this is no fairy tale. David, where is your Deliverer now?

The people following David are so "bitter in soul" (v. 6) that they talk about stoning him! At this point, I might be the one to cut bait and run, but that's not how David responds.

When things look desperate, when the stakes are high, and when the dangers are great, David doesn't look at the terror, the flying arrows, or destruction. Instead, "David strengthened himself in the LORD" (v. 6). Yes, David lives out his faith—he looks to God amid devastating loss. He inquires of the Lord, and God guides him to pursue the Amalekites. Ultimately, David rescues all the women and children that had been captured (see v. 18).

How might you and I be strengthened in the Lord as we face life's hardest circumstances?

I love that this story has a happy ending, but friends, you and I have an even better ending. Why? Because God sent His Son, Jesus, to be our strength and our ultimate deliverer.

We have Jesus, who says, "Peace! Be still!" (Mark 4:39) to calm a storm.

His disciples asked, "Who then is this, that even the wind and the sea obey Him?" (Mark 4:41) You and I know that this man is our Messiah.

Jesus spoke peace then, and He speaks peace now as we worry over finances that threaten to ensnare us. Jesus speaks peace in the face of a pandemic. He speaks peace in the places of our lives that feel overtaken by darkness and uncertainty. Jesus speaks peace even as we watch the world get rocked by wind and overtaken by waves of hate and division.

As we encounter bleakness—the loss of a job, a cancer diagnosis, debilitating depression, the struggle to get pregnant, the loss of our precious loved ones—we can weep until we have no more strength to weep. But we do not "grieve as others do who have no hope" (1 Thessalonians 4:13). Instead, we can strengthen ourselves in the Lord as we look to the peace we have in Jesus.

"Peace! Be still," daughter. Jesus, who conquered death and sin, is your strength and shield.

Rest without Guilt

I f you're like me, you have an endless to-do list: work, family, house, church, and community responsibilities. One task is completed only to be replaced by another. It's satisfying to check something off the list, but that feeling is fleeting. I never feel on top of things.

Recently, I had an afternoon without work or kids. It crossed my mind to read a book, maybe a fun novel. I fantasized about reading on the padded couch in the screened porch and sliding into a nap.

But it's only 2:00 p.m. on *Monday*.

I immediately felt guilty and anxious about the fantasy. *I'll drink some iced tea to perk up. Then I'll organize the garage.* That task is on my to-do list; reading for fun and napping are not. In fact, reading and napping sound lazy, even indulgent.

Why does the thought of rest trigger this reaction in some of us? Why do we equate "not actively working" with laziness and indulgence? Perhaps it's cultural, as many people value a strong work ethic. Perhaps our role models displayed achievement through constant motion. Perhaps people we know use jokes to shame others for relaxing activities. Perhaps we fear the to-do list will never get done.

But perpetual busyness is a trap. It's possible that when we are busy, we feel needed, important, and relevant. Busyness is a source of pride and a part of our identity. We have status when we are in demand. But maybe we've confused being busy with true productivity. Maybe we are checking tasks off our lists without fulfilling healthy priorities. We are our own worst enemy when we allow pride to overtake our need for rest. God even commanded us to rest on the Sabbath (see Exodus 20:8), and Jesus regularly took time alone to pray, reflect, and recharge (see Luke 6:12, for example).

Imagine you are super fit, hitting the gym multiple times a week. You don't exercise the same muscles each day though. You operate on the knowledge that your body recovers more quickly and builds muscle more efficiently when you take time off between workouts. Similarly, God wants us to rest so we can be rebuilt in Him. He wants us to trust that He is in control and we can do nothing without Him. His wings are our refuge (see Psalm 91:4). Indeed, God strengthens us while we rest because our strength is not enough.

Sadly, many of us don't receive enough of the primary restful activity—sleep. Other restful activities include walking, gardening, meditating, hiking, cooking, getting a massage, and praying. When we rest, our brains are free to solve big problems. Negative emotions are easier to keep in check. We build a reserve of energy to draw upon when needed, and we experience a boost in the feel-good endorphins that assist our overall well-being.

It's hard to shift away from an unyielding, achievement-oriented daily structure. But rather than give in to old habits of busyness, we can develop new habits of rest.

We don't have to pressure ourselves to be perfect or constantly work toward earning God's acceptance. In fact, we can't do this. Our sinful human nature, our short-sighted choices, and our focus on the to-do list all put us in the number one position. It's as if we are saying that all things depend on us. But the truth is that nothing about our standing with God depends on what we do. We can't be on enough committees, go to church often enough, or pray enough to complete the work God has given us to do. Only Jesus can do that.

Jesus completed every task required to satisfy the work we need to fulfill God's purpose for us. Jesus accomplished this work perfectly and completely. And because we can be confident in what Jesus has done for us, we can fully rest. We can set aside our job, housework, or family for a while to recharge and refuel. We rest fully when we focus on God's Word for us. We receive nourishment and calm in the Sabbath rest of worship and we receive the Lord's Supper.

Trust God's promise to carry all your burdens and protect you (see Psalm 91:3–6).

God is my comfort and my trust,

My hope and life abiding;

And to His counsel, wise and just,

I yield, in Him confiding.

The very hairs, His Word declares,

Upon my head He numbers.

By night and day God is my stay;

He never sleeps nor slumbers. (LSB 758:2)

Freedom of Feeling

D anger! Beware! Often, it feels like life should come with a warning. Psalm 91:3–8 names a host of perils: snares, pestilence, terror, darkness, destruction, and arrows. We probably will not have to worry about actual arrows, but we deal with personal challenges every day. Sin, self-doubt, excessive worrying, temptation, and selfishness are dangers that can turn our focus away from our Savior.

But this psalm gives us hope for life's challenges. He paints a beautiful picture of God's protection. In our most difficult times, we are reminded that God gives us refuge and a safe place where we will find comfort and solace in our Father's arms. We can be certain that He is always with us, and we are never alone, just as we know that Jesus' death on the cross and His resurrection offers us grace and redemption. In our worst times, we have peace, hope, and certainty that He is our "shield and buckler" (v. 4), and we know He covers us with His pinions. We find refuge under His wing. What a wonderful gift, and how great His faithfulness!

God's providence eases fear, doubt, and worry. Feeling free from worry lightens our hearts and opens us up to seek opportunities to care for others. The promise of God's protection is not just for you and me; it is a promise for all God's people. Philippians 2:3–5 says,

> Do nothing from selfish ambition or conceit, but in humility count others more significant than yourselves. Let each of you look not only to his own interests, but

also to the interests of others. Have this mind among yourselves, which is yours in Christ Jesus.

My focus diverts from my worries and fears to joyfully sharing God's faithfulness and protection. I have the freedom to share the peace, hope, and love of Christ. We are all called to love the least of these, the hurting, and the lonely. It becomes a joy to provide care, compassion, and kindness to others when we consider the unconditional love our Savior extended to us in His death on the cross. Our love and gratitude for our Father compel us to consider the needs of others. Just as our Father does for us, our hearts ache for the pain of others. We feel compassion when we consider the loneliness of others. We want to share God's love and protection and offer hope and God's comfort.

Prayer: Heavenly Father, thank You for Your promise of protection from all I encounter. I pray that I seek You as my refuge and solace, my place of comfort. I pray that my life would honor You as I strive to be selfless and consider others before myself because I can be sure of Your faithfulness. In Jesus' name. Amen.

My Shield and Buckler

P salm 91:3–8 is filled with vivid word pictures. Imagine the Lord providing shelter for you as a mother bird's wings—feathers puffed up, spread out, surrounding her chicks, and pulling them close. Although this brings to mind warmth and security, what's emphasized here is the protection from danger that is yours in Christ. The psalmist elaborates further with war imagery: "the terror of the night" and "the arrow that flies by day" (v. 5) describe life in this sinful world for what it is: a 24/7 day-to-day battle with Satan, the world, and our own sinful selves. You've seen it, haven't you—the darkness of disaster and disappointment, ready to strike when we least expect it?

Years ago, I remember feeling envious of people who had an inspiring faith story to share. I had a beautiful family and wonderful friends but had never faced adversity enough to challenge my faith. Then unexpectedly, cancer invaded, attacking my father, husband, and son within several years. The offensive wasn't only against the flesh and blood of my loved ones but also against confidence in God and firm trust in all His promises.

God's faithfulness truly was a shield and a buckler (a smaller shield held by hand or worn on the forearm) during this vulnerable time. Whether I felt it or not, I was held safe behind the formidable "shield of faith" (Ephesians 6:16) gifted to me at my Baptism. But just as chicks must stay near their mother's protecting wings to be safe, I had to cling to the "sword of the Spirit, which is the word of God" (v. 17). I held my buckler against the blows of every diagnosis, struggle, and even death.

I remember devouring Scripture and writing it in a notebook as I prayed the words of God over my son during his brain surgery.

I committed Scripture to memory and relied on it as I put on the face of outward calm in doctor's offices, praying for the terror inside to recede. Through those years, I was never alone. God spoke through family, friends, and strangers who sent cards and emails with Scripture verses. I strapped these on against incoming threats, taping them to walls where I would see and remember. Personal messages of hope in the words of prayers or hymns were timed just right for my ears. I vividly remember sitting in church and "praying" the verses of the hymn "Christ Be My Leader," as well as these familiar words from "Abide with Me":

> *Abide with me, fast falls the eventide.*
> *The darkness deepens; Lord, with me abide.*
> *When other helpers fail and comforts flee,*
> *Help of the helpless, O abide with me.* (LSB 878:1)

Life is hard. Being a Christian does not guarantee you will be protected from hardships and disappointments. But you *will be* protected *as life takes you through those things.* The arrows and night terrors you feel might not be health-related. The pestilence of this world is not limited to the attacks of cancer, viruses, or physical struggles. It also lays siege with temptations of worry, doubt, self-pity, and anger.

Wars, natural disasters, and pandemics do not discriminate. You might know first-hand that job loss, broken relationships, and dysfunction are not limited to unbelievers. But *know more and trust this*: when life is under attack, "our God whom we serve is able to deliver us" (Daniel 3:17). When you feel alone and fearful, stand firm behind the shield of God's faithfulness, reach for the buckler of God's Word and His promises, and remember the One who loves you and says, "Fear not, for I have redeemed you; I have called you by name, *you are Mine*" (Isaiah 43:1, emphasis added).

Having It All

H i, I'm Kristan," the smiling stranger said as she video-chatted with me from her vacation home nestled in the mountains of Colorado. I tried not to raise my eyebrows as I surveyed her massive house.

Weeks later, freshly installed at my new job at her church, I found myself perched on the couch in Kristan's gigantic living room at her *other* house, in Texas.

Despite her warm hospitality, I didn't know what to think of her.

Kristan had it all: a doting husband, a high-powered job, two darling kids, an enviable closet, and two beautiful houses. On top of that, she was an active member of our congregation and school, serving joyfully in several volunteer roles while wearing killer shoes I could never afford.

My chagrin melted the more I got to know her, however. One day, as we sipped tea together, I asked how she did it all.

"What do you mean?" she replied, staring at me over her cup.

"All of this," I answered, waving my hand at her house. "Your house is impeccable, your kids are well-behaved, and you manage to look perfect even though you work a busy job. How do you do it all?"

"This takes a lot of work!" she laughed, crinkling her nose. "I have a full-time nanny and a housekeeper. I could never do this all on my own!"

People tell themselves a lot of lies about their happiness. We whisper that we'll be happy if we can just get that next thing: a degree, marriage, a career, a baby, a new car, a kid on the honor roll, that purse, or that house in that neighborhood.

Scripture reels us back to the truth that lasting contentment and true peace are found in Christ alone, not in our possessions, accomplishments, or relationships. As Psalm 23:1 reminds us, "The LORD is my shepherd; I shall not want."

The truth? Kristan's life isn't perfect. Neither is mine. Neither is yours. We all struggle with plenty of heartache in this broken world.

That's why we so desperately need a Savior. Safe in His arms, we find true peace. We can face whatever the world throws at us with confidence knowing that we are forgiven children of the King, welcomed into His family through our Baptism.

My life will never be perfect, and I'll certainly never have the beautiful homes and shoe collection that my dear friend Kristan has. But I can hold myself back from the frenzied pursuit of perfection by knowing that my life is good because I am richly blessed by God. My journey is unique. So is yours. And instead of drowning in the misery of discontent and bitter envy, we can rest securely in God's love, which provides all we need.

Psalm 91:4 tells us, "He will cover you with His pinions, and under His wings you will find refuge; His faithfulness is a shield and buckler."

We are nestled securely into God's protection, and His care for us is evident when we count the blessings in our lives. Through Christ's redeeming love, our past no longer haunts us, our present circumstances allow us to be content, and our future doesn't need to scare us.

When Kristan proclaimed, "I could never do this all on my own!", she declared the refrain of all of our lives. We could never do life all on our own without our Savior. We desperately need Jesus, the forgiveness He offers, the hope He extends as we walk through the darkest valleys.

I could never do this all on my own—and thank God I never will.

Death's Sting Is Lost Forever

The light was on in the room; that was a sure sign she was awake and might be receptive to a visit. Peering inside, I could see that she was looking at a crucifix on the wall while slouching in her hospital bed. On the table was a straw with a sponge on the end so she could wet her chapped lips; it was obvious she could no longer eat solid food.

As I washed my hands before entering her room, I heard her speaking. It was not a whisper, but a conversation, even as her voice would go in and out. I could tell she was saying something she had memorized, and it was not until I heard the words that I knew for sure what she had been reciting:

> A thousand may fall at your side,
>
> ten thousand at your right hand,
>
> but it will not come near you. (PSALM 91:7)

It was obvious that she had not just learned this psalm, and this was not the first time she had prayed it. "My grandmother taught it to me," she explained as she turned to face me when I approached her bed. In the palliative-care ward of this hospital, honest conversation about the past, present, and future often were the norm, so she shared her story with me during the final days of her gallant battle with cancer.

By no strength or merit of her own, it was clear in our conversation that day that the Holy Spirit had called her, enlightened her, and sanctified her in the one true faith. The crucifix at which she gazed was a perfect reminder of exactly how God rescued her from the enemy—through the death and resurrection of Jesus Christ, our Lord. It would never matter how many people around her fell since neither the arrows of the accusing enemy nor the destructive pestilence could ever harm her. She was baptized into the death and resurrection of Christ Jesus. We rejoiced that on the Last Day, Christ will raise us from the dead and we shall see the recompense of the wicked since, in Christ, "Death is swallowed up by death, its sting is lost forever. Alleluia!" (*LSB* 458:4).

Although others may think it ironic, we shared with each other that, even in a sterile palliative-care room, deliverance from a deadly pestilence is a promise fulfilled in Christ. It is this kind of faith that motivates us to sit up wherever we are and face our battles head-on. The sure and certain promises of God revealed to us in His Holy Word keep our eyes squarely on the crucified Christ and give us strength and peace to face anything, even earthly death.

A few days later, as I arrived at the time of my friend's death, the light in her room was dim. At her bedside, I recited that psalm once more, remembering not only what her grandmother taught her but also the faith we confess as the Church Triumphant.

In His mercy, our Lord delivered her from the snare of the fowler. Under His wings, she found refuge—His faithfulness was her shield and buckler, her dwelling place, her refuge. What was true for the psalmist is true for us.

The Everyday Trials of a Bird

Whoa! Birds. There is a deliberate focus here in Psalm 91:3–8 that is absolutely wonderful because of its simplicity for the reader. The more I pore over this passage, the clearer this story of hope unfolds in my mind. The psalmist is relating us, as God's children, to the everyday trials of a bird. Ha! The prevalence of birds in our lives as civilized human beings is not lost on me here. How easy it is for us to understand this childlike comparison and then build upon it as we seek to understand God's presence, role, and the way He works in our lives more.

Check out how the powerful lyrics of "Consider How the Birds Above" (*LSB* 736) support this theme! "He will deliver you from the snare of the fowler. . . ." "He will cover you with His pinions," "and under His wings you will find refuge" (vv. 3–4).

A bird that is being hunted by a fowler, dodging arrows that are meant to take it down, daily threatened with pandemics (pestilence) and deadly disease, the sweet sparrow is one of many birds that live in fear of the unknowns of life—the things it can't prepare for, such as attacks by the enemy, sickness, disease, and destruction.

And we, sweet sisters, are likened to the sparrow (see Psalm 84:3; 102:7; Proverbs 26:2; Matthew 10:29, 31; Luke 12:6–7).

Just as a fowl flees from the "arrow that flies by day" (v. 5) as it watches thousands of fellow birds fall, so we are reminded by Martin Luther that if we could see how many knives, darts, and arrows Satan and the sinful world have aimed at us, we would gladly come to the Sacrament of the Lord's Table—the shadow beneath the wings—as often as possible. Under His wings, we live in hope and have protection.

But how? How does this hope happen in the shadow of the Almighty? By Jesus Christ alone. Jesus' body and blood renew our bodies upon eating and drinking for spiritual battle. Jesus is the Word (see John 1:14) who speaks guidance and wisdom and discernment into all the unexpected transitions we go through in relationships, friendships, locations, vocations, maturity, health, and experiences. In our Baptism, Jesus covered us with His mighty wings. We are chosen, adopted, redeemed, forgiven, loved, and known by Him through the washing of these worn little feathers at the font.

Last but not least, Jesus is the forgiveness of our sins. Dwell in the shadow of the Almighty and receive the forgiveness He gives not by your own doing but by the mercy and the grace He lavishes upon us. This forgiveness is the only remedy for the crisis of conscience and the guilt that separates us from Him and from one another. A guilty conscience keeps us from entering the shadow of protection and keeps us vulnerable, dodging the arrows that fly by day and the pestilence that stalks us by night.

> He will cover you with His pinions, and under His wings you will find refuge; His faithfulness is a shield and buckler. (PSALM 91:4)

So where do we find the shelter of the Most High then, sisters? In the Divine Service, where God serves us everything we need to get through life. Jesus, tangible Jesus, is giving Himself to you in every situation you're facing today and tomorrow. He is always drawing us closer to Him and teaching us how to be more like Him in the secret place under His wings.

I'm the Worst Climbing Partner

And the LORD will guide you continually and satisfy your desire in scorched places and make your bones strong; and you shall be like a watered garden, like a spring of water, whose waters do not fail. (ISAIAH 58:11)

I swallowed hard as I scrolled through the trail map. "Will you do it with me?" my husband asked.

One interest that C (my husband) and I share is hiking. However, my style of hiking is different from his. I prefer the kind of hike where I am prepared for anything but can be safe the whole time—a well-marked trail, a challenging but safe hike. C, on the other hand, lives for anything difficult. When he hikes, he takes the bare essentials and goes as light and high and fast as possible. The kind of adventure where people say "I could never do that!"

C had always wanted to hike Angels Landing in Zion National Park. Google it when you get a chance. It is considered one of the most dangerous trails in the United States. I didn't know much about the trail when he brought it up. But when I looked into it, I was not surprised that he wanted to do it.

This trail was completely out of my comfort zone, but it was important to C. Marriage is about sacrifice, right? So, sacrificing my comfort, we hiked Angels Landing.

We set out when it was early morning and shady. At first, it didn't look so bad. There were several switchbacks with a gradual incline. But after the switchbacks, the trail climbed higher and narrowed down to an 18-inch-wide ledge. On one side, there was a rock wall with grab-chains bolted into the rock. On the other side, there was . . . nothing. By the time we got to this point, it was sunny and 110 degrees. There was no shade, no water, and no relief. In the most literal and blunt sense: you fall, you die.

I was terrified, hot, exhausted, thirsty, and numb. Yet C

* ❈ held my hand, even when I crushed his so hard we both thought I broke his fingers;
* ❈ encouraged me though I did not encourage him;
* ❈ talked me through when I was white-knuckling the chains;
* ❈ carried our sixty-pound pack the whole time;
* ❈ said we could turn back whenever I wanted;
* ❈ never gave up on me and never complained; and
* ❈ gave only grace and love beyond what I deserved.

I'm the worst climbing partner, but my husband invited me to hike with him that day and made it possible for us to complete the trail together. I still don't know how we got to the top, but I'm glad we did. The view was incredible, and the sense of accomplishment was gratifying. And that climb taught me something new, I think, about God's way of whispering into the depths of my heart to let His faithfulness be my shield (Psalm 91:4).

Life gives all of us more than we can handle on our own. The dangerous trails and narrow climbs are terrifying. But God provides everything we need for the hike. In His Word, He gives us the chain to hold onto and the encouragement to take the next step. He never promised life would be easy, but in the person of His Son, He promises to be with us always and to carry our weight.

Whatever climbs you face, let His faithfulness be your shield. Let His Word guard your heart with the promises of Jesus, reminding you that His death is your life. His grace and mercy are glorified in the mountains He has called you to climb. His Sacraments sustain you and remind you of His mercy and grace when you falter. May the climbs in your life draw you into deeper dependence on the One who is always faithful.

Living God, Your almighty power

is made known chiefly in showing

mercy and pity. Grant us the fullness

of Your grace to lay hold of Your

promises and live forever in Your

presence; through Jesus Christ, Your

Son, our Lord, who lives and reigns

with You and the Holy Spirit,

one God, now and forever.

(COLLECT FOR PROPER 27, SERIES C)

Personal Reflection

*Because you have made the L*ORD *your
   dwelling place—*

   the Most High, who is my refuge—

no evil shall be allowed to befall you,

   no plague come near your tent.

For He will command His angels concerning you

   to guard you in all your ways.

On their hands they will bear you up,

   lest you strike your foot against a stone.

You will tread on the lion and the adder;

   *the young lion and the serpent you will
   trample underfoot.*

PART 3

Psalm 91:9–13

AUTHORS:

Rosie Adle
Janine Bolling
Jessica Bordeleau
Jessica Brashear
Connie Denninger
Carol Fedewa
Noemi Guerra

Sarah Gulseth
Rehema Kavugha
Katie Koplin
Courtney Limmer
Megan Mertz
Kathy Pingel
Barbara Shippy

True Rest

In the center of Psalm 91, we are reminded, perhaps not to our liking, that the world is full of threats and trials like sickness and stones, lions and snakes. No psalmist has to work too hard to persuade us that life is tough and quite often terrifying.

In the past, the mention of a "plague" may have conjured blurry images of biblical or historical hardships experienced by other people, but now the word lands close at hand. A stone might remind you of a pesky pebble in your shoe, or it could call to mind a downright boulder in your path, blocking you from the dream that won't come true. The language in this psalm can wiggle you into your weary place where the ravaging beasts of life snarl right in your face.

But even as this reel of evil rolls, the psalmist puts these troubles in the context of the refuge you have in the Lord. To call the Lord your dwelling place is to recognize that His presence has a permanence in your daily life. It makes room for you to see the evil around you as powerfully painful in the here and now, yet powerless to separate you from the love of God in Christ Jesus.

These words from Psalm 91 are not a lucky charm that can shoo away sickness, excavate rocks off the path, and lock up lethal creatures for good. They are words that assure you that even as the trials of life may exhaust and dismay you, you are not overcome, and you are never alone. You dwell with the Lord; He dwells with you.

God is at the heart of all you experience, putting His own dear Son, Jesus, between you and every rock and hard place you face. It doesn't mean the boulders get blown to fairy dust.

Instead, it means that the stone was rolled away from the empty tomb to show you your new life in Christ.

The promised Savior first mentioned in Genesis 3:15 is with you this day. He sees the threats upon your life, whether physical, spiritual, emotional, or mental, and He dwells with you. Not one of the present afflictions can separate you from the love of our Lord. Not one! This offers true rest from fear and failure.

Prayer: Most High God, whose Word and Sacraments strengthen me to face attacks and whose angels protect me from dangers here below, guard me for the moment when they will bend to earth with a new purpose: to bear me up to the dwelling You've prepared where no evil will befall me, that I will receive by grace the gifts of eternal life with Christ, as He lives and reigns with You and the Holy Spirit, one God, now and forever. Amen.

Moving Is Stressful

O pening prayer: Holy Spirit, be with us as we read the words of Holy Scripture. Calm our hearts, open our minds, and help us to hear what You have to say to us from the Psalms. Amen.

How many times have you moved in your life? The average American moves eleven times. For me, that number is seventeen. Each time I move, whether it is where I live or where I work, I learn something new.

At Our Saviour Lutheran in the Bronx, New York, we moved teaching and office spaces twice during the same summer due to contract changes and a natural disaster (Hurricane Ida). Both moves happened with short notice and both were mentally and physically stressful. It took a lot of work to remember that God was beside us and guiding us.

Moving is stressful, and when you do it alone, the packing, lifting, shifting, organizing, and getting settled sometimes seem insurmountable. Worrisome questions pop into your brain. *Will this place ever feel right to me? Will I fit in with my neighborhood? Did I make a huge monetary deposit somewhere that I won't have peace?*

Moving can also cause you to ponder what "home" really is. In Psalm 91:9, we see that "you have made the LORD your dwelling place." This is a powerful reminder of the God who remains beside us, fighting evil and calamity on our behalf. In a world that feels dangerous and uncertain, *He* is our dwelling place. In a city that feels lonely, *He* is by our side.

It is difficult to move and settle into a new place. That difficulty intensifies when doing it alone. I moved ten times before age 30, and I was single. Each time, I faced the challenges of making decisions, trying to fit in, and getting used to a new place alone. Our world can feel like a couples culture, and being part of a couple is a blessing from the Lord. But not being in one has its own set of problems. This is where clinging to Scripture is necessary.

You may recall the account of Jesus being tempted by Satan in Matthew 4. Psalm 91:11–12 is a foreshadowing of Satan's mocking of Jesus: "For He will command His angels concerning you to guard you in all your ways. On their hands they will bear you up, lest you strike your foot against a stone." Satan tried to use this verse for evil, but Jesus could not be turned. The truth of God's Word prevailed. Later in the account, we read about that promise being fulfilled: Satan fails, and the angels attend to Jesus.

The promises of God are true for us as well. The Lord Most High is our dwelling place, wherever we may be. Whether we are moving states, cities, houses, apartments, or shelters, or we are simply having a mental move or shift, God is there. While we were still sinners, Christ died for us so that we may have the One who remains at our side through the worries and stress, showing His love and care and making His home with us. May you remember the One who abides with you as you move through the seasons of life. You are never alone.

Prayer: God of our refuge and strength, when things are shifting, help us remember that You keep us grounded. We pray for Your continued guidance in our lives, and we thank You for the gift of Baptism where You make Your home with us. Amen.

He Holds Fast

"Mom, I got hurt!" Amid tears and bloody knees and shivers down your spine, you get the bandages. Sound familiar? Last month, my son fell at a park. He wandered around the playground looking for me, holding his broken wrist to his chest. When I got to him, he collapsed in my arms, sobbing. "It won't stop hurting!" All I could do was try to comfort him as we drove to the doctor.

Our heavenly Father knows what it's like to see His children suffer. From broken bones to broken hearts, He sees our pain and knows our feelings. Unlike an earthly parent who watches helplessly, He is all powerful. He can do anything. Scripture speaks to God's ability to keep His people safe. Psalm 91:10–12 says it clearly:

> No evil shall be allowed to befall you, no plague come near your tent. For He will command His angels concerning you to guard you in all your ways. On their hands they will bear you up, lest you strike your foot against a stone.

If God can keep us safe, why do we still get hurt? It's tempting to think that He must be too distant to notice our cry or worse—that He just doesn't care. Satan used that same verse to tempt Jesus:

> Then the devil took Him to the holy city and set Him on the pinnacle of the temple and said to Him, "If You are the Son of God, throw Yourself down, for it is written, 'He will command His angels concerning you,' and 'On their hands they will bear you up, lest you

strike your foot against a stone.'" Jesus said to him,
"Again it is written, 'You shall not put the Lord your
God to the test.'" (MATTHEW 4:5–7)

The devil tried to twist the meaning of God's words, but
Jesus wasn't fooled. When we go through suffering, it isn't a
test of God's love for us. His love for us is steadfast despite the
hurt we endure in this life. God doesn't immediately deliver us
from pain and hurt in this life, but He sent His Son, Jesus, to
give us ultimate and eternal deliverance. Jesus could have called
angels to deliver Him from the cross, but He didn't. He bore the
weight of our sin and willingly took what we could never bear.

When we face suffering, we may feel like my son did when
he fell: confused and alone. We wander in pain, searching for a
pair of strong arms to hold us. Unlike a human parent, who can
give comfort but not healing, our heavenly Father gives both.

> When the righteous cry for help, the LORD hears and
> delivers them out of all their troubles. The LORD is
> near to the brokenhearted and saves the crushed in
> spirit. (PSALM 34:17–18)

When Jesus returns in glory, God's angels will bear us up.
Every stone, rock, and boulder that stands between us and God
will be removed. We will never stumble, fall, or suffer again.

> He will wipe away every tear from their eyes, and death
> shall be no more, neither shall there be mourning, nor
> crying, nor pain anymore, for the former things have
> passed away. (REVELATION 21:4)

That day is certain, and it is coming. Until then, we have
the assurance that the Lord walks with us through the tortures
of this life. He holds us close as we cry out to Him. He gives us
comfort and strength to make it through. Just wait—the day of
deliverance is coming!

God Knows Exactly Where You Are

The sun was setting on a day full of vacation memories. I sat peacefully on the pebbled beach, digging my hands deep into the tiny, charcoal-colored pebbles around me. I ran my fingers in swirled patterns, marveling at the unique makeup of the spot. I picked up a handful of the perfectly smooth stones for closer inspection, and a lone white pebble caught my attention. I stared at the contrasting stone, perplexed by its oddity among the rest on the beach and wondered *Why is this one white? Where did it come from? How did it get here?*

Then, just as quickly as my pondering began, I realized that God knew exactly where this white rock had originated. He knew how it had traveled to that exact spot for my hand to pick it up. That tiny rock reminded me of His omniscience and omnipresence in my life.

Have you ever been the white pebble—alone on a seemingly endless beach of charcoal? Have you ever been isolated, lonely, or asking yourself, *How did I get here?* Sometimes loneliness is physical, and other times it is a state of mind. We can be surrounded by people and feel completely alone. Perhaps you have felt like a small stone tossed by an ocean of violent waves. Waves of failed relationships, broken friendships, miscarriages, deaths of loved ones, infertility, empty nesting, economic hardships, and personal insecurities crash down. Such waves beat us up and spit us out. We feel tossed and turned, exposed and fending for ourselves on an unfamiliar island named Loneliness.

While we are tossing and turning, Satan whispers, "You're all alone." He plants seeds of insecurity that sprout into fears of loneliness, leaving us crippled by our inabilities. Truthfully, we are incapable because of our humanity but never alone because of our capable God.

Satan might be whispering, but Christ's death and resurrection assure the believer that the king of lies has been defeated. Jesus promises in John 14 that the Helper, the Holy Spirit, dwells and lives within us. Satan's whispers will fall on deaf ears when we turn up the volume of that truth.

Psalm 91:9–13 reminds us that the Lord is our dwelling place and our refuge. He doesn't promise that the violent waves won't come, but He does promise to be our sheltering guard and to send angels to concern themselves with our safety. Matthew 28:20 reminds us, "And behold, I am with you always, to the end of the age." We are never alone because there is no space or time that He doesn't go with us. His saving grace and mercy envelop us. He promises to *never* leave or forsake us (see Deuteronomy 31:6).

Friend, if you are hearing the whispers and feeling the waves, find courage and security in your faithful Father. He sees exactly where you are. He knows where you've been. He knows where you're headed. He knows it and walks it with you. When you can place your assurance in His omniscience and omnipresence, the waves fall flat, the whispers go silent, and loneliness is tamed.

Prayer: Lord, calm my waves and fill my heart with Your company. Keep Your angels close and silence the whispers that pull me from You. I trust in all Your promises and lean not on my feeble understanding. Provide me with a community of Christ-followers to encourage and point me back to You. Lord, with You, I am never alone. In Christ's name. Amen.

My Refuge and Dwelling Place

Our modern culture loves to use superlatives to designate winners and the best. Connecting with that makes us feel like we make the grade somehow, perhaps even leaning toward "untouchable." Yet during the COVID-19 pandemic, we marked pitfalls of loss with so much left undone or swept aside. Feeling like we have lost out is common. Maybe this virus has come near us. We may have suffered the loss of family members or friends. Maybe the illness has even befallen us. It becomes easy to feel like evil lurks everywhere and has managed to invade our homes and impact our lives. Our lives have felt unprotected, vulnerable, and out of control.

When I was twenty-four years old, I lost my first husband to Hodgkin's disease. I truly felt that the world had crumbled and that my life was in shambles. But my Baptism promise of God's faithfulness helped slowly rebuild my trust in His provision. Even when I wasn't faithful, the Lord was faithful to me. God sent caring helpers to guide me, and in time, the dwelling place of the Lord was again my safe, sheltered place. It wasn't an instant or easy fix, and there were many days I was simply held by the Lord. I have clung to His promise in Psalm 91:11 many times: "For He will command His angels concerning you to guard you in all your ways." The Lord sends His angels for *me*. I am important enough to be in the watchful eye of the Most High God. My sorrows, loss, shattered dreams, and even death itself are not beyond the power of His hand over my life. The healing and outcome of good health for my husband was not the ultimate plan for my life, but God brought that hardship into goodness as my life is worked out in His ultimate creation of renewal.

The mysterious and profound work of the Holy Spirit has always been in my life. I am protected by the hands that bear me up. Most High God—now that is a superlative I can count on. When I remember that His presence is my dwelling place, I set aside time to be in His presence. That strengthens me when I feel weak and weary, as I am called to abide with Him. It brings hope and healing in situations where I have no control. Every breath is known by my powerful God, and He loves to be in relationship with me and remind me that when I seek Him as refuge, there is no evil that can snatch me from His hands.

My confirmation blessing verse is John 10:27–28. Jesus says, "My sheep hear My voice, and I know them. . . . And they will never perish, and no one will snatch them out of My hand." That becomes my place to rest and respond to His great love for me. Since I am a visual, kinesthetic learner, I often create reminders of these biblical truths and set them around my house to see daily. I may add journaling notes in my Bible or draw a prayer card in response to reading God's Word. Simple exercises like these help me remember His ultimate plan of salvation for me through His Son, Jesus.

That gift of grace calls me to give thanks for this promise of refuge now and right into His eternal kingdom.

Faith Is for Sharing

For as long as I can remember, I have believed in God. Having been born into a faith-filled family, God was a given. From the time God called me into His glorious grace through the waters of my Holy Baptism as an infant and throughout Sunday School and confirmation as a teen, God was a constant in my life. I knew He loved, cared for, and protected me.

As I matured, so did my faith. I began to spend regular time in God's Word, ingesting His truths and promises through good and challenging times. During this time, God revealed a deeper understanding of His character and His gifts of grace, love, forgiveness, and hope. He drew me closer into a personal relationship with Him, and in response, I wanted to know Him more and walk in His ways. Today, I cherish the relationship I have with my Savior and all of the ways He has grown my faith. He continues to call me to grow even further in my faith and serve Him in my life—in particular, sharing Him with those who do not believe.

Typically, my days have me walking among other believers. My job, extended family, friends, and church life all include other believers. In these areas, I can freely share my love for the Lord and rejoice with others as He lives and moves in our lives (see Philippians 1:6). Very little of my time is spent with nonbelievers, other than encounters at the grocery store, doctor's office, or elsewhere. In these places, opportunities abound for me to share Jesus with others. Yet I rarely do.

I know that God wants me to be out among those who do not yet know Him. Jesus Himself came for the sick and sinful, not the healthy and righteous (see Luke 5:31–32), and He sent

His apostles out into the world to spread the Gospel. But it's easy to get comfortable, even complacent, staying among those who believe in and follow Christ. It's convenient to say that God calls others to do the work of bringing nonbelievers to Christ. It's painless to leave the work to someone else. But the truth of the matter is that God calls each of us to discipleship, which includes sharing the truth of our Lord with those who do not know Him.

This needn't be difficult. We make our attendance at church and participation in church-related activities a priority. We bring our offerings, which support the work of our local congregation and may extend to mission work elsewhere. We pray that the Lord would guide our words and actions so that everything we say and do points to Him—whether we are within our comfort zone or outside it.

Through the Holy Spirit's work within us, we are equipped to convey all of God's goodness and faithfulness. We sow the seed; the Lord makes it grow. Every encounter becomes an opportunity to live out our faith and spread the hope of heaven.

Is God calling you to share Him with someone who does not believe? Yes, He is. As believers, we have been given an incredible gift of faith. With this faith comes the responsibility to bear witness to our Lord and Savior. When we do, the Holy Spirit works within their lives to guide them from unbelief to faith. Then God is glorified, lives are changed, and our own faith is strengthened.

Prayer: Father, thank You for the gift of faith and for opportunities to share with others the life and sacrifice of Jesus so that they, too, may know the way to eternal life with You. In Jesus' name we pray. Amen.

The Black Hole

There is a dark place I fear in my house. Like a black hole, it's deep and quiet and so treacherous! It is . . . that space between the cushion and the bottom of my living room recliner. It's deep, but it doesn't reach the floor. So if something falls into it . . . it disappears! It is lost forever! I told y'all it was dark and scary!

To be honest, I think I have fallen into that space myself—the space between the cushions of society and the church. I may be lost forever!

You see, I am what is called a 1.5 generation Latina (an immigrant who came to the United State at age 18 or younger). Some first-generation Latinos think I am a "traitor" because I learned English and went to college. Some second-generation Latinos pity me because of my accent and feel "responsible" for teaching me how to get rid of it. *It's not happening* (says my brain with a thick accent)! And, of course, the non-Latinos have no clue 1.5s even exist! Can you see me between the cushions?

It doesn't stop there. The church has its own cushions, and many of us have fallen into the space between them. Have you ever felt like you aren't praying enough, aren't pious enough for your church friends? Have you ever found yourself saying "churchy" words with your "wicked" friends and blushing? If so, you may be a 1.5 Christian. You may have fallen into the hole of how the world expects a Christian woman to be versus what she actually is.

Well, sister, embrace your accent! I mean your dark place. Being a Christian woman doesn't mean that you will never sin or that you are exempt from the dangers of this world. Sometimes you will find evil befalling you, plague coming near your tent, and that you are striking your foot against a stone. But know that you are protected amid all of it. You are not lost forever. You are a saint and a sinner, born again in the waters of Baptism and strengthened in the Lord's Supper. Jesus conquered the grave and bridged all the space between the cushions for us.

It's often in the space between or the dark and lonely places that God does some of His greatest work. If no one else understands you or sees you in this space, be assured that Jesus does. He knows what it's like to be forgotten, cast aside—He even went through the darkest of places for us so that we would be brought into the light.

But until He comes back in His glory and takes us home with Him, remember that amid every hole you fall into, God has commanded His angels concerning you—to guard you in all your ways, to protect you and carry out His will in your life, to bring you to the place He has prepared for you. On their hands, they will bear you up with His Word as a lamp to your feet, lest you strike your foot against a stone of doubting your future in Him. You will tread on the lion like Daniel did and the adder like Paul did. The young lion and the serpent of demonic terrors of the dark you will trample underfoot because He has given you strength in His Word and Sacraments. He has given you authority when you face spiritual warfare and divine protection and power over demons in your Baptism.

Now pray with me in the accent you've always had: Father, thank You for sending Your holy angels to be with us. Thank You also for sending church workers, pastors, parents, friends, teachers, and doctors. We are victors and survivors in You; You are in our midst. In Jesus' name and for His sake. Amen.

Our Priceless Treasure

How are you doing, dear sister? Are you feeling the weight of the world? Take a deep breath with me, and sing these beautiful words from Johann Franck (translated by Catherine Winkworth):

> *Jesus, priceless treasure,*
> *Fount of purest pleasure,*
> *Truest friend to me,*
> *Ah, how long in anguish*
> *Shall my spirit languish,*
> *Yearning, Lord, for Thee?*
> *Thou art mine,*
> *O Lamb divine!*
> *I will suffer naught to hide Thee;*
> *Naught I ask beside Thee.* (LSB 743:1)

Our spirits languish quite often these days with many demands on our time. If you feel like you're being pulled in a million directions in any given hour, you're not alone. Our vocations of sister, daughter, mother, wife, friend, employee, citizen, etc., require us to manage our time, and when those requirements become overwhelming, we are left with languishing spirits. It's easy to slide into feelings of guilt and shame when we are faced with these obligations because we want to be all things to all people. If we agree to a volunteer activity for church, for example, we may have to decline a coffee date with a friend. In these moments, we feel defeated and guilty for letting people down. But sister, there is a better way.

In Thine arms I rest me;
Foes who would molest me
Cannot reach me here.
Though the earth be shaking,
Ev'ry heart be quaking,
Jesus calms my fear.
Lightnings flash
And thunders crash;
Yet, though sin and hell assail me,
Jesus will not fail me. (LSB 743:2)

In these moments when sin and hell are assailing us with needless guilt and shame, we look to Jesus. Remember your Baptism, dear sister! In our identities as children of God, washed clean in Christ's blood, we are free to serve our neighbor. We are also free to set boundaries and tend to our mental and physical health. It is not physically possible to be all things to all people. But Jesus never fails us. In Him, we have grace upon grace (see John 1:16), and we come to Him with repentant hearts in our weakness and failings to receive His abundant mercy and forgiveness.

Satan, I defy thee;
Death, I now decry thee;
Fear, I bid thee cease.
World, thou shalt not harm me

Nor thy threats alarm me
While I sing of peace.
God's great pow'r
Guards ev'ry hour;
Earth and all its depths adore Him,
Silent bow before Him. (LSB 743:3)

As baptized children of God, we can tell the devil and his minions that we belong to Christ. What power we have in those words! We come before Christ each week to receive Him in Word and Sacrament, bowing before Him in awe and wonder at His bountiful goodness to us. The world cannot harm us, and Satan cannot touch us. Our God will guard us in all our ways!

Hence, all fear and sadness!
For the Lord of gladness,
Jesus, enters in.
Those who love the Father,
Though the storms may gather,
Still have peace within.
Yea, whate'er
I here must bear,
Thou art still my purest pleasure,
Jesus, priceless treasure! (LSB 743:6)

So while we wait for our Lord Jesus to return, we will inevitably be faced with troubles and temptations, fear and sadness in this fallen world. We cling to our priceless treasure, Christ Jesus, knowing that He guards and protects us in this life.

We have the peace of God that surpasses all understanding (see Philippians 4:7).

Prayer: Lord Jesus, You are my priceless treasure. Give my spirit peace when I am languishing. Forgive my sins and keep me in the true faith until You return! Amen.

Jesus Is My Dwelling Place

D o you remember being scared as a little girl? Do you remember being so scared that you just needed to grab hold of someone or something? The thing I needed to hold was my bear, Lamar. I still keep him nearby at night. Over many years, he has given me a sense of security. Will Lamar save me from anything? No. But I feel better knowing I can snuggle with him.

Did you ever think about wrapping your arms around Jesus? Like that print of Jesus welcoming the children that probably hung on a wall in your Sunday School class, our Lord is always there with His arms wide, ready to welcome you. In Psalm 91, the relationship is even deeper. You go to Jesus not only for a hug but also for your dwelling place—your place of refuge. How does that make you feel?

The Lord is *your* dwelling place. When the storms of life are swirling all around you—when the questions of doubt, fear, loss, and so much more overwhelm you—seek refuge in Him. He promises that "no evil shall be allowed to befall you, no plague come near your tent" (v. 10).

Take comfort and strength in that promise.

Do evil things happen? Do we as Christians suffer pain and death? Yes, but God is sovereign. Because Jesus has defeated death and the devil, He will not ultimately allow evil to befall us, for He has delivered us from that end through the mercies of Jesus. Psalm 91 says He will not allow evil to befall us and His angels will bear us up so we do not strike a foot against a stone (vv. 11–12). God gives us His angels and our sisters in Christ on this earth. Who are those women for you? Who are the ladies in your life that you can turn to in times of sadness and joy? Are they women who remind you of whose you are and turn you back to Jesus?

As I have gotten older, my friend group has changed. I still have a few close friends from high school and college that I stay in contact with, but over time, I have learned that I need to surround myself with women who point me to Jesus and the Gospel.

The struggles of life continue to get bigger and bigger, and our world has become unrecognizable. It is so easy to get swept up in the chaos of this world and to feel utterly alone. Sometimes we cry into the darkness of the chaos, waiting for a response that never comes. The reality is, I know I can always speak to Jesus, but I do not always remember to do so. Do you know who does? My friends. They point me to the light of Christ that helps me out of the darkness.

It is in those moments that I am reminded that my identity is in Christ and that He is my dwelling place. Then I hear God's words calling me to Him, and I remember that His angels are surrounding me. That brings me great joy.

When the storms of life swell up around you and the chaos of culture seems to overwhelm you, surround yourself with friends. But most important, surround yourself *in* Jesus, who is your dwelling place.

Prayer: Heavenly Father, I thank You for being my dwelling place. Amid my life and the chaos of this world, may I remember to seek refuge in You. Surround me with Your holy angels to guard and protect me. And thank You for my sisters in Christ who surround me daily and point me back to You. In Jesus' name. Amen.

Our True Dwelling Place

For the first seven years of our marriage, we lived in a two-bedroom house in the middle of nowhere, North Dakota. During those seven years, it became our place of refuge. The longer we stayed, the more adamant I was about staying. I even thought about being buried in the cemetery a quarter-mile from our house.

We worked hard to make that two-bedroom house our dwelling place and our refuge. We replaced damaged windows. My parents gifted us flooring for our wedding, and it was laid in the heart of the home—the kitchen. I gave gardening many hearty attempts. We ate from the already established asparagus patch each year. At our patio door, we watched crops being planted and harvested in the field behind our home.

We worked hard to make a community for ourselves too. We hosted Bible studies and potlucks. Each year we celebrated birthdays with friends and relatives, and as years passed, the relationships we nurtured with neighbors, co-workers, and fellow church members deepened.

After all of that work, it was hard to say goodbye to that dwelling place. It was hard to say goodbye to the home we had done so much growing in. It was harder to leave the people we had worked to forge relationships with. The house had become our dwelling place, our home, and so had the people.

We moved four years ago when our jobs changed, but we are busy with the same type of work. We work on our home and our community. As my parents say, the work of a homeowner is never done. Weeds pop up in the landscape. Dandelions take over the grass. Large trees die and need to be removed.

Gutters fail and basements flood. The constant demands of life often create more chaos than peace.

Amid this work, we read Psalm 91:9–13 and are reminded where our true dwelling place is:

> *Because you have made the LORD your dwelling place—*
> > *the Most High, who is my refuge—*
> *no evil shall be allowed to befall you,*
> > *no plague come near your tent.*
> *For He will command His angels concerning you*
> > *to guard you in all your ways.*
> *On their hands they will bear you up,*
> > *lest you strike your foot against a stone.*
> *You will tread on the lion and the adder;*
> > *the young lion and the serpent you will trample*
> > *underfoot.*

Life's circumstances change, and the places we live are altered. But our dwelling place with the Lord is secure. We will work on a home and in a community to make it a refuge, only to leave it behind. But our dwelling place and the refuge we find in Christ never leave us behind.

While the work of a homeowner and neighbor is never done, the work required to dwell with Jesus is complete. There will be dangers and drama no matter where we make our home, but He will command His angels to watch over and protect us. Jesus walked through the wilderness and encountered all the dangers and temptations that come our way. He guards our ways and commands His angels concerning us. On the cross, He crushed the head of the serpent. Our dwelling place is secure because of the work He has done.

Prayer: Lord Jesus, as we work in our homes and communities, grant us the knowledge that we are secure and safe because of who You are. Regardless of place or circumstance, remind us that our dwelling place with You is secure. Amen.

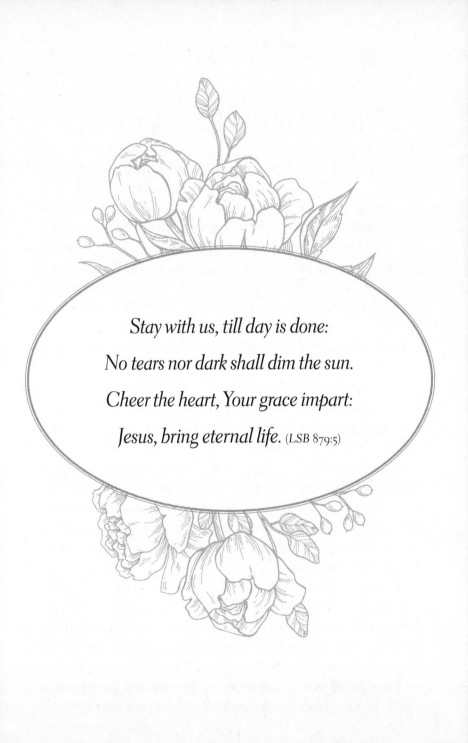

Stay with us, till day is done:

No tears nor dark shall dim the sun.

Cheer the heart, Your grace impart:

Jesus, bring eternal life. (LSB 879:5)

There Are No Easy Answers

When I was a junior in college, studying to be a director of Christian education, I thought I knew it all. I felt so ready to serve a congregation with my wealth of theological knowledge—until a professor stumped me with a question in class. This class was all about teaching Christianity to teens, and my professor posed as a student grilling us with questions. "What does Psalm 91:10 really mean?" he challenged. "Is God actually promising that He'll protect us from all harm? What does that mean if something bad does happen?"

I fumbled to find the right answer. "Maybe this is saying no evil will befall us spiritually," I said.

My professor raised an eyebrow. "That's a big assumption. That doesn't seem to be what the passage implies," he said.

I suddenly realized two things. First, there are no easy answers to the questions this passage raises. Second, I didn't know as much as I thought I did. It was a humbling moment, and it led me to think more deeply about what Scripture says.

In the years since that class, I've often pondered Psalm 91 and my professor's questions about it. At times, I've asked a similar question myself: *Why does God allow evil to befall people when He clearly says He won't?*

I know it is foolish to try to understand all of God's ways with my finite human mind. Isaiah 55:8 reminds us that God's ways and thoughts may not make sense to us but are ultimately better than our own. There's comfort in knowing that someone much wiser and stronger than me is in control.

I also know that God is good. Scripture is full of verses that proclaim His goodness. A quick internet search can direct us to hundreds of Bible passages that do just that. God is also the source of good, the one who defines what is good. Surely we can trust Him to determine what is truly best for each of us.

And of course, the Bible reminds us that God is not only good; He is also love (see 1 John 4:8). He loves His people so deeply that He sent His own Son, Jesus Christ, to take the penalty of our sins upon Himself, die excruciatingly, and rise again so we could have a restored relationship with Him (see John 3:16).

God also claimed us as His family through Baptism. We know that no matter what happens to us, we are His, and He is a good Father who loves and takes care of His children. He also surrounds us with the rest of His family—our brothers and sisters in Christ who support and encourage us, who preach the Gospel and teach us.

It's been several years since that class, and I see Psalm 91 reflected in my life and ministry. Through the best of times, the spiritually dry seasons, and the times of deep pain, God has been with me. He's been constant and faithful and has given me hope, peace, and joy. He has surrounded me not only with His angels (see Psalm 91:11) but with the family of God—mentors advise me in my ministry, friends lift me up in prayer, and my family encourages me when I'm struggling. God, in His goodness and love, guides me as I serve, helping raise up a new generation of people who know Him.

Now, as I walk my students through their own hard questions, I point them to our dwelling place, the One in whom we trust even (and especially) when we don't have all the answers.

Great Expectations

Throughout the 1990s and 2000s, TV sitcoms taught us that by age 25 or so, we'd have a swanky New York City apartment, a successful career that offered plenty of free time, and a close-knit group of friends who were always up for brunch. Things like marriage and family would fall easily into place at the perfect time as well.

But life doesn't always go like we expect or hope or as sitcoms would have us believe. Today, twenty-five-year-olds may still be living with their parents and may feel lonelier than ever. A study conducted in October 2020 by the Harvard University Graduate School of Education found that 61 percent of people aged 18–25 experienced significant loneliness. The COVID-19 pandemic may have exacerbated this, but it wasn't the only cause. The meteoritic rise in dating apps and infertility treatments point to the truth that getting what we want most of all isn't guaranteed.

Our social media feeds, filled with perfect pictures—snapshots of smiling children, a high school classmate's successful business, or Instagram-worthy photos from a friend's exotic vacation—add to this malaise. All these things can make us feel inadequate—as if we don't measure up.

As much as we might sometimes wish, God is not like a fairy godmother. He doesn't wave a magic wand to fix our problems. He doesn't promise that our lives will be perfect or easy. In fact, He promises quite the opposite. Jesus said, "In the world you will have tribulation. But take heart; I have overcome the world" (John 16:33).

Just look at Jesus. God did not spare His own Son from hunger or ridicule or even a brutal death on the cross. He was abandoned by His friends and suffered the most gut-wrenching pain and humiliation. Yet through that suffering and death, Jesus saved the entire world, including you.

When we are overwhelmed with disappointment, regret, or desperate longing, the Lord calls us to cast our cares on Him and make Him our dwelling place. "Because you have made the LORD your dwelling place—the Most High, who is my refuge—no evil shall be allowed to befall you, no plague come near your tent" (Psalm 91:9–10).

That doesn't mean the Christian's life will be smooth sailing. In this life, we will suffer. We will not always get what we want, even if it's something we want desperately. Worst of all, we will suffer not just because of this world or the evils around us; our own sin condemns us before God and causes suffering in our own lives and the lives of our loved ones.

But we can take comfort in God's promise that He will be with us, even when we don't see Him. Jesus' death and resurrection forgives our sins and reconciles us with God and one another. And finally, on the Last Day, we know that we will not be forgotten. Jesus will call us forth from the grave—leaving behind all the frustrations and disappointments of our mortal life—to live in His presence forever.

Look for the Blessings

H ave you ever wondered why the Lord allows bad things to happen to good people or why it seems like God is helping everyone else but you? I think a lot of us have felt that way. We have wondered *Where is God in this?* Or *I am a Christian. I do the best I can. I repent of my sins. I receive Holy Communion. I am a baptized child of God. God loves me and cares for me. So why aren't things happening the way I think they should?*

Well, as we look to Scripture for God's truths, He reminds us that believers are not exempt from trouble. He also assures us that He has us in the palm of His hand. Friend, there is no safer place to be.

When I question God or wallow in self-pity, I know it's because I haven't sought God's direction. I have searched for answers I thought were right, but perhaps that answer wasn't best for me or others.

God answers us in the way and time that are best according to His will for us. He desires all people to be saved. He wants all people to come to the knowledge of Him and the salvation He freely gives through the death and resurrection of His Son. His answers are always best.

But problems will come our way. Satan continuously tries to pull us away from God and trick us into thinking God doesn't care about us, especially during rough times. But Satan lies. God's Word tells us, "He will command His angels concerning you to guard you in all your ways" (Psalm 91:11). God uses the problems in your life for good and to draw you closer to Him. Romans 8:28 says, "And we know that for those who love

God all things work together for good, for those who are called according to His purpose."

Your heavenly Father loves you so much. He wants you to know that you are His child. He reminds you of His love and forgiveness through the gifts of His body and blood through Holy Communion, the cleansing waters of your Baptism, and the gift of His Word.

I bet when you look back at rough times in your life, you will see God's blessings—people who have come to your aid and reached out with words of encouragement, a prayer, a meal, or simply their presence. Those were the hands and feet of Jesus reaching out to you. He loves you, and that love led Him to take the punishment for all our sins to the cross, where He endured ultimate pain and suffering. There, He defeated sin, death, and the power of the devil that we might be saved.

Because of Jesus, the pain we now experience is only temporary. Amid struggles in this life, be assured that God sends His angels to surround you and protect you. He sends the Holy Spirit to be with you and strengthen you. He loves you beyond measure and promises that neither "height nor depth, nor anything else in all creation will be able to separate us from the love of God in Christ Jesus our Lord" (Romans 8:39).

So while you wait patiently for Him to do what is best, be still and know that He is working all things for your good.

That's a promise you can count on.

God Is with Us in the Valleys

I n January 2015, my husband and I moved seven hours away from family and friends for his new job. That alone was challenging. But in addition to life in a new city, his job required travel about 80 percent of the time. This new season presented unexpected challenges and exciting opportunities that, in the end, balanced each other out. It was like we were walking along a plateau.

Then came the valley.

That fall, I received a phone call from my doctor after a routine checkup. After the call, I remember staring at the notes I had taken and wondering how to tell my husband, who was on a business trip, what I had learned—that there was a very good chance I had cancer. Later that night, I received another call, the one I had been dreading for years. My dad was calling to say it was time to come home because my grandmother wasn't doing well. I always knew the close relationship Granny and I had was special, something to be treasured. But such closeness also comes with a steep price when the relationship is gone. Several days later, Granny passed away—hours before my first appointment with the oncologist. All we could do was marvel at God's timing of these life-altering events. After some time, we praised God for a cancer-free diagnosis. But months later, we received another one: unexplained infertility.

> *Because you have made the LORD your dwelling place—*
> *the Most High, who is my refuge—*
> *no evil shall be allowed to befall you,*
> *no plague come near your tent.* (PSALM 91:9–10)

When Christians experience hardship, we can either scoff at God and His Word and His promises or make the Lord our dwelling place—lean into Him and His Word, trust Him fully, and walk in faith.

Psalm 91:9–10 is not assuring us of an affliction-free, danger-free life, as it might seem at first glance. Rather, the psalmist is assuring us that amid affliction and danger, God will never abandon us. In fact, "He will command His angels concerning you to guard you in all your ways" (v. 11).

When it feels like all that surrounds us is evil, and all that comes near our tents is plague after plague, it can become challenging to believe in our hearts what we know to be true in our heads—that God is good, and His will is perfect. And so we make Isaiah 55:8–9 our refrain:

For My thoughts are not your thoughts,

neither are your ways My ways, declares the LORD.

For as the heavens are higher than the earth,

so are My ways higher than your ways

and My thoughts than your thoughts.

As I write this, my three miracle boys are napping in their rooms across the hall. I am still cancer-free, and while I miss my grandmother dearly, I treasure the photographs that pop up on our digital picture frame and hearing my four-year-old exclaim, "That's Granny!"

My journey through that particularly long valley has come to an end. But in the years since, my husband and I have journeyed through others—and I know there are more to come. The same is true for all believers. But you and I can take heart and be not dismayed, for God will strengthen us, help us, and uphold us with His righteous right hand (see Isaiah 41:10).

Personal Reflection

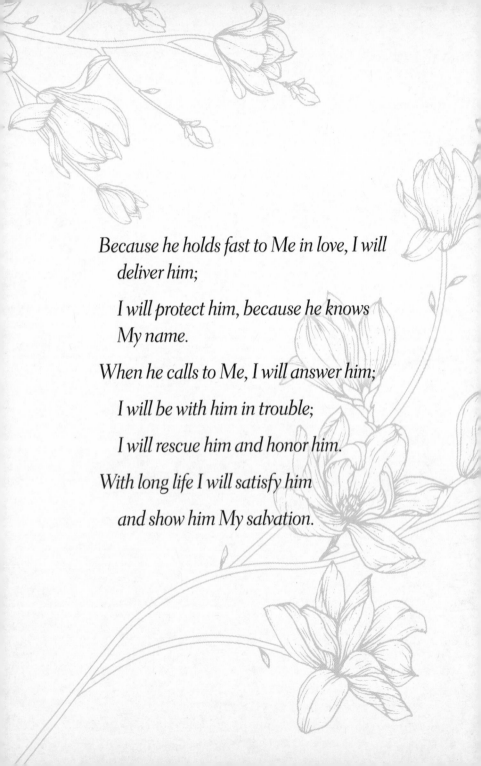

Because he holds fast to Me in love, I will
  deliver him;

  I will protect him, because he knows
  My name.

When he calls to Me, I will answer him;

  I will be with him in trouble;

  I will rescue him and honor him.

With long life I will satisfy him

  and show him My salvation.

PART 4

Psalm 91:14–16

AUTHORS

Rachel Bomberger
Heather Choate Davis
Michelle Diercks
Catherine Duerr

Pa Her
Molly Lackey
Tiffany Manor
Julianna Shults

He Holds Fast

What amazing promises these words from Psalm 91 contain: an answer to every prayer and protection in every trouble—deliverance and rescue, honor, long life, companionship, and salvation—all straight from the hand of the Lord God Almighty. Who wouldn't want these good things in their life? What a deal! Yes, please!

Yet when I read these promises in context and note the conditional statements that go along with them, I can't help but feel a shudder of doubt.

"Because he holds fast to Me in love, I will deliver him" (v. 14, emphasis added). But do I *really* hold fast to God?

"I will protect him, *because he knows My name"* (v. 14, emphasis added). How well do I *really* know His name? Such knowledge, I fear, is too wonderful for me.

Isn't this always the way it goes? I encounter a beautiful passage in Scripture—one full of hope and strength, comfort and triumph—and instantly make it all about me. I read the story of David and Goliath and immediately identify with David. I read Joshua, and I'm Joshua; Ruth, and I'm Ruth; Esther, and I'm oh-so-obviously Esther. I read Jesus' parable of the sower and—*boom*—just, like that, I'm the sower. The protagonist. The hero. That's me.

I read the Psalms, and I just assume every lament, every promise, every righteous rant, every holy utterance, every blessing—those words are all obviously mine, right?

Somewhere along the way, though, this me-centric hermeneutic always breaks down. Verses like Psalm 91:14 show me why. My faith is weak; my wisdom is paltry. If perfect trust and deep knowledge are required to unlock these wonderful blessings from God, I am disqualified. Completely ineligible. I'm a poor, miserable sinner. I have "sinned against Him in thought, word, and deed, by what I have done, and by what I have left undone." Whenever I make *myself* the hero of the story, the whole thing falls completely apart.

But what if I am not the hero of the story? What if I read these verses again and consciously recognize *Christ* as the hero? Suddenly, it all works. Seen through Christ—through His life, death, resurrection, and ascension—everything becomes clear and comes together.

Because Christ held fast to His Father in love, God delivered Him. Because Christ knew His Father's name, God protected Him. When Christ called out, God answered Him. God was with Him in trouble. God rescued Him and honored Him. With eternal life, God has satisfied Him and shown Him His salvation.

The sinful part of me feels just a twinge of regret at this, like the older brother in the prodigal tale. *Why does everything always have to be about Jesus? Why is it never about me?* It stings my pride to know that, on my own, I am never worthy.

Thanks be to God, I never have to read these verses on my own. I am baptized into Christ. I partake of His very body and blood at His Table. His life is my life. His faith is my faith. His story is my story.

"All the promises of God find their Yes in Him" (2 Corinthians 1:20). His promises are certain, unchanging, and true because Jesus fulfills them. When we call upon God in Jesus' name, He answers us. Hidden in the folds of Christ's righteous robe, we find rescue and protection, long life, and satisfaction. In Him, we truly know the joy of God's salvation. With Christ as our hero, God's promises are all for us.

Prayer: Thank You, Father, that all Your promises find their yes in Christ. Help us trust Him as the true hero of our story. Deliver and protect us and show us Your salvation for Jesus' sake. Amen.

The Living God

To arrive at the final lines of Psalm 91 is not simply to hear the psalmist wrap things up with a few lovely "in conclusion" thoughts—no. To reach these final verses is to stand on the rare and holy ground of one of the most powerful salvation oracles in sacred Scripture. Nowhere else in all of the Psalms does God make so many promises in such a compact proclamation—seven of them, to be exact. Seven first-person-singular promises spoken by the Lord Himself to each of us through the psalmist.

> *Those who love Me, **I will deliver**;*
>> ***I will protect** those who know My name.*
> *When they call to Me, **I will answer** them;*
>> ***I will be with** them in trouble;*
>> ***I will rescue** them and honor them.*
> *With long life **I will satisfy** them*
>> *and show them My salvation.* (vv. 14–16 NRSV)

In the centuries before "the Word became flesh and dwelt among us" (John 1:14), the Jewish faithful would sing this psalm as they went about their day. They knew God's promises intimately because His Word had become part of their pulse and breath through song and repetition. Today, this practice carries over into liturgical worship with the use of an antiphon (sung refrain) repeated throughout the psalm reading, echoing our Old Testament roots. I learned the ancient practice of psalmody at a Benedictine monastery at age 33, only months after coming to faith. It has been an integral part of my daily prayer life ever since.

Twenty-five years later, God built on that formation. Although I couldn't play an instrument, read music, or even carry much of a tune, I started "hearing songs." Soon I knew I was being called to use music to speak to people about the beauty of a life lived in Him. As I pondered the fullness of these two lines of the psalms, I was not surprised when I "heard" this sung refrain: "I am and I will, I am and I will, I am and I will. Be still."

In this simple utterance, we are reminded of whom the living God is: "I AM WHO I AM" (Exodus 3:14). "I am the way, and the truth, and the life" (John 14:6). "I am the true vine" (John 15:1). "I am the Alpha and the Omega" (Revelation 22:13). Then, on this sure foundation, we add His promise to act on our behalf: I will. These seven promises will never be broken. These are seven promises we can hold fast to when the ground beneath our feet feels like it's slipping away. Be still. It's not a command but an invitation. Let Me help you, comfort you. Let Me deliver you from this dark season and into an even more marvelous light.

So let's pray these lines now together in the name of Jesus. If you can read music, great. If not, just move your voice up and down in your best imitation of Gregorian chant. First, we'll sing it one time through. Second, we'll read verse 14, followed by the antiphon. We'll do the same for verses 15 and 16.

I Am & I Will
An antiphon for Psalm 91:14-16

music & lyrics by
Heather Choate Davis

When you're done, you may want to go back and use this antiphon throughout the whole of Psalm 91. (You can break it up every two verses, or just after vv. 2, 8, 13, and 16.)

As you begin to embody His promises through this sung devotion, you might even find that the words have become your own, and you are now able to offer them back to your Creator in perfect faith: I am trusting in You. I am abiding faithfully in Your love. I will be still. Amen.

Peace I leave with you; My peace I give you. I do not give to you as the world gives. Do not let your hearts be troubled and do not be afraid. (JOHN 14:27)

Our Sabbath Rest

Perhaps, like me, you feel you have everything under control—until you don't.

One evening, I was talking to my husband, Troy, who had been sick for most of the day. As he was talking, his words came to a sudden stop, and he slumped over in his chair. I touched his shoulder and spoke his name; he gave no sign of awareness. I raced to call 911. In distress, I launched words of panic into the dispatcher's ear when Troy called out, "I'm okay." Relief poured over me, and I canceled the 911 call. We took him to the ER by car. Diagnosis: Troy was dehydrated and weak from being ill. As I think about those moments of uncertainty, I'm certain God sheltered us in the shadow of His wings.

We don't get to dictate the troubles that come into our lives; they will come no matter what we do. But we cannot function in a continual state of fear and worry, anticipating the trials and tribulations and trips to the emergency room. So what should we do?

God commands us to cling to Him. Some passages tell us to abide in God (see John 6:56; 15; 1 John 2:27). The word *abide* conveys a place where we rest in Him.

Where do you find rest? Between the hurry-sick and worry-sick moments, where can you rest your heart?

For many of us, there are roadblocks to finding this place. Our thoughts about obligations, relationships, hurts, griefs, and grudges get in the way. We try to bear these burdens on our own, and it exhausts us. This is when we need to sit and take a few moments to consider our troubles. And what to do about them.

The only real way through the maze is to ask Jesus to help you untangle your thoughts and emotions; He is the shelter and the guide. As you do this, remember that you sit in the shadow of the Most High and can be confident in these promises:

- ❋ Peace is found in the refuge that is the promises of Jesus in His Word. Let Jesus take your burdens. They are not yours to carry. Firmly place them into His most capable hands.

- ❋ Jesus welcomes you to surrender your burden. Place your confidence solely in Him to take care of it, and rest your full weight on His promises.

- ❋ Jesus will deliver you from your hurry and worry.

- ❋ Jesus will protect you and rescue you in each moment.

- ❋ Jesus will always answer you.

Jesus saved you from your most significant problem: sin. Salvation is already yours through Him. This is not a someday promise; it is a right-now promise delivered to you through your Baptism. Your Baptism isn't a distant event; it is a daily event, renewed by the power of the Holy Spirit.

> But when the goodness and loving kindness of God our Savior appeared, He saved us, not because of works done by us in righteousness, but according to His own mercy, by the washing of regeneration and renewal of the Holy Spirit, whom He poured out on us richly through Jesus Christ our Savior, so that being justified by His grace we might become heirs according to the hope of eternal life. (TITUS 3:4–7)

As you attend the Divine Service and receive the Lord's Supper, the gifts you are given there continue beyond the service because they are Christ's work within you, and He strengthens your faith. The rest you receive on the Sabbath continues throughout your week and cannot be taken from you because Jesus is with you. He is your Sabbath rest.

Junior High Scars

I n junior high, I was part of a group of friends. We hung out before school, ate lunch together, and walked around, talking. We had sleepovers and other gatherings. One day, with no warning, some of the girls found me alone before school. One looked me straight in the eye and said, "We don't want you to hang out with us anymore."

I was devastated. That day, and many more days, I ate by myself in the cafeteria, stood by myself before school, and cried over the missed sleepovers. The rejection affected how I behaved. I became withdrawn, insecure, and shy. And the emotional scars stayed with me.

In an unrelated event, or so I thought, I decided to start going to church. I had been baptized and we went to church a few times a year, but now I felt compelled to go more regularly and learn more about the faith. So my mom signed me up for confirmation class—about a year and a half *after* the class had started.

I walked into a room of confirmands, the new girl in a place where everyone knew everyone. The first person I saw was Charlie, a notorious bully from my school. Sitting with him was Chuck, the stepbrother of one of the girls who had kicked me out of their group.

This didn't look good.

Whether it was due to the setting, the presence of the pastor, or the passage of time that brought maturity, I didn't experience any of the harassment or intimidation I expected. Charlie left me alone; we never even exchanged words. Chuck, on the other hand, became one of my best friends.

I learned a lot in confirmation class. I began going to worship services every week and participating in activities. I flourished at church. During my high school years, I had a lot of friends and was elected president of the youth group. This was where I was home, loved, and accepted. This was where God wanted me—in His house to learn about Him and share my faith with others.

This sense of belonging has stayed with me. But sometimes, even all these years after junior high, I still struggle, wondering if people are genuine or if they will reject me. Then I remind myself that what matters is that Jesus loves me and does want me around. He made that abundantly clear by dying for my sins and failings so I could be saved and spend eternity with Him. I am home in Christ's Church on earth. It's where God comes to me in His Word and Sacraments. It's where I'm forgiven and fed and loved unconditionally through Christ. He will never reject me, never leave me.

I recently wrote a Bible verse on a sticky note and put it on my refrigerator: "The LORD your God is in your midst, a mighty one who will save; He will rejoice over you with gladness; He will quiet you by His love; He will exult over you with loud singing" (Zephaniah 3:17). It makes me smile to visualize God singing over me. No matter how lonely the world may make me feel, I know I'm not alone. My best friend is the "mighty one who will save."

Prayer: Dear Jesus, I am nothing and have nothing to offer You. But You love me anyway. You have made it known to me that You are with me always and You have given me the ultimate gift. You died so I could be with You forever. And because of You, I am something. I love You. Amen.

Hold Fast to Him in Love

You have probably heard the phrase "the American dream." When somebody appears to have everything—a well-paying job, a caring family they can support, a home they love, and money left over to make life enjoyable—they are said to be living the American dream. Many people work hard all their lives to chase the American dream. Some have even immigrated to the United States in pursuit of it.

As a daughter of immigrants, I hoped that one day I could achieve the American dream. I studied, got good grades, graduated, and landed an awesome job. After getting married, my husband and I had children, bought a house and a minivan. Through our hard work and dedication to the goal, we were on our way to achieving the dream. That is why, when my husband brought up the idea of attending Concordia Seminary to become a pastor, I saw my carefully created world start to crumble.

It wasn't until we packed what belongings we didn't sell or give away and moved our family five hours away to the seminary that I started to question the empty promises of our previous life, the pursuance of an earthly dream. I started to see that these promises distracted us from living a faithful life dedicated to God.

The simple life we led at seminary gave us a new commitment to family activities, more time for family devotions, and time to join Bible study groups. With the previous focus on the American Dream, the focus on ourselves, our house, and our busy life had led us away from focusing on God, focusing on prayer, and fixing our minds on God in all things. The American dream is an empty promise that leads to disappointment and discontent. It is a constant chase of the latest trend, the newest thing. Our eternal, unchanging God promises to take care of us, a promise we can trust—a promise that has been fulfilled through Christ.

In Psalm 91:14–16, we read God's promises for those who hold fast to Him in love. Here, God makes eight promises to us: to deliver, protect, answer, be with in trouble, rescue, honor, give long life, and show His salvation. To whom are these great promises made? Simply put, they are made to the one who trusts in God: "I will say to the LORD, 'My refuge and my fortress, my God, in whom I trust'" (Psalm 91:2).

Through your Baptism and the Lord's Supper, God's promises are fulfilled. You are saved! You can truly trust God's Word of mercy, forgiveness, and salvation. God's love for us, fulfilled in Jesus, is no dream that we are in pursuit of. It is only truth that is ours, now and forever.

No Matter How Lonely

And behold, I am with you always, to the end of the age.

(MATTHEW 28:20)

We find ourselves in a world of ever-increasing loneliness. We feel lonely because we don't talk to our neighbors, don't get along with our family, can't get out as much as we used to, are busy with work, are busy with kids, are unable to find work, are unable to have children. Everyone is so busy, so angry, so hostile—including ourselves—and our struggles with sin only make the problem of our isolation worse. It makes us want to scream. But will anybody even hear us?

Yes. God, your Father, Creator of the universe and your very body and soul, says yes. "When he calls to Me, I will answer him; I will be with him in trouble; I will rescue him and honor him" (Psalm 91:15). Our Lord hears our prayers, Holy Spirit-enabled cries for help, aching, and groanings too deep for words (see Romans 8:26). But how can we be sure? It certainly doesn't feel like God is listening when our prayers for a friend, for reconciliation, for peace, for health, for work, a husband, a child, or for *anyone to notice us at all* seem to go unanswered.

But this prayer has already been answered in Christ. Jesus comes to you and says, "I will . . . show him My salvation" (Psalm 91:15–16). The very Word of God, who spoke every single subatomic particle into existence out of nothing, took on frail human flesh, endured stress, sadness, pain, and, yes, even loneliness, to show you His salvation. He calls to you with outstretched arms from the cross. The Lord of lords also knew loneliness as the Roman scourge fell across His blameless back, as the nails pierced His sinless hands, and after His disciples had forsaken Him and left Him to bear the mockery and hatred of the world, as He breathed out His life-giving breath in the gasp of death. He suffered all this shame, pain, and loneliness for you.

In this psalm, God promises that "because He holds fast to Me in love, I will deliver him; I will protect him, because he knows My name" (Psalm 91:14). Maybe in the throes of our loneliness and pain, we are struck by how we don't deserve this salvation. We have forgotten the very name of our Lord. But Jesus hasn't. Jesus is the deliverer in this psalm, the perfect Son who died and rose from the dead to deliver us from our enemies.

This applies to you in your Baptism when you are marked with the name of Christ and redeemed from sin, death, and all suffering. And even in the face of all sorts of evil, torment, sin, and loneliness, God will never forsake you. Not now, not ever. No matter how alienated you feel from your friends, family, the world—and maybe even yourself—there is nothing that can separate you from God's love for you or from Jesus (see Romans 8:39).

Knowing God's Name

God speaks blessing to His people. He made you His own in the waters of Baptism when you received life and salvation in His name. He spoke blessing and forgiveness to you then, and ever since, God has been with you, delivering and protecting you. In Psalm 91:14–16, God is speaking, promising multiple blessings to those who know His name.

Knowing His name, knowing the true God, is the most important thing you will ever know. God's promises in this psalm and all of Holy Scripture are for those who know the truth. This truth gives you protection and more: "And this is eternal life, that they know You, the only true God, and Jesus Christ whom You have sent" (John 17:3).

God has caused you to know the truth, to know His name. He has blessed you with life and salvation. He also has prepared you to be a blessing to the people He has sent to you through your roles or vocations in life. As He formed you in your mother's womb, you were created a daughter. In your Baptism, you were made a sister in Christ to all the saints in His Church. You were also made a neighbor to the people He puts in your path. He might also give you other special family callings in life, such as niece, aunt, wife, mother, or grandmother. In every one of these vocations, God gives you people to serve and reflect His love upon as you care for them in body and soul. Living out your vocations and loving the friends and family members that God has given you is joy, a fruit of the Holy Spirit given to you in your Baptism (see Galatians 5:22).

Serving in your callings is joyful in Christ, yet the joy is often mingled with struggles and hardship (see James 1:2).

He promises that in all of your vocations, He will be working through you, strengthening and sustaining you through His Word and Sacraments. "He who calls you is faithful; He will surely do it" (1 Thessalonians 5:24).

God tells you what He will do in Psalm 91:14–16. He first promises to deliver and protect you. He adds to His safeguarding of you with His promise of continual presence and answers to your prayers. The Lord is with you in trouble. He rescues and honors you. In addition to those abundant blessings, the triune God—Father, Son, and Holy Spirit—gives you satisfaction in eternal life and salvation.

Prayer: Heavenly Father, I give You thanks and praise for making me know Your name and for all the blessings You pour out on me. Be with me to strengthen and sustain me as I love and care for the people You have given to me so that they would know the love of God found in Christ Jesus, who lives and reigns with You and the Holy Spirit, one God, now and forever. Amen.

The World Is Not as It Should Be

One of the things I love best about working with young people is that they are always discovering new things about the world and themselves. It is a gift to watch them take new information and turn it over in their minds. They sometimes surprise themselves with what they can do, and they challenge the status quo in beautiful ways, especially in the church.

But times of discovery often lead to realizations that the world is not as it should be. The perfect world God created in Genesis 1 has been wrecked by sin, death, and the devil. It is painful to see passionate, empathetic young people discover the dark, troubled chaos in our world, hypocrisy in people they admire, and broken systems that perpetuate fear and hurt. I wish I could protect them, but honestly, as I watch the news and scroll through social media, I can still be shocked by the trouble, sin, and pain that impact our world today too.

Praise God that His Word doesn't skip over the trouble in our world. It is honest about how our broken world can be filled with evil, pestilence, darkness, and fear. Scripture also points us back to God's perfect love, promises, and presence.

Psalm 91 starts as a confession of faith in God, who is a refuge and protector through all the trouble of our world. The last three verses of the chapter, however, shift into God speaking promises to us. We hear words we need when hope wanes and the world feels like a chaotic dumpster fire.

God promises to hold fast to us in love. Death, destructive weather, disease, and conflict can shake our confidence and loosen our hold on faith in God's goodness. But we don't have to worry if our grip is enough to hold onto God because it doesn't depend on our strength. God holds us confidently on the solid rock of our salvation. God's deep love clings to us as we navigate all we experience and discover in life.

God hears our cries and knows us each by name. Through our heartbreak, sobs, and the times when we don't know what to say, God is near us. We long to be seen and known. God promises His presence is not far away; He is close enough to count the hairs on our heads. God walks with us and, through the Holy Spirit, uses us to shine Christ's light into the darkest of places.

Through Jesus, we have a God who offers salvation, rescue, and protection. God has overcome sin, death, and the devil through Jesus' perfect life, death, and resurrection. Even when we bring trouble on ourselves, break relationships, and cause pain, we repent and find forgiveness. No matter how bad this world may get, we know God has promised us salvation, forgiveness, and everlasting life.

We can't protect young people or ourselves from sin and brokenness. On this side of heaven, we will continue to feel distressed as we discover darkness and trouble in the world. But just as He promised, Jesus has conquered all. We can find hope, comfort, and rest in God's good gifts.

God holds fast to us, walks with us, rescues us, and protects us so that we can face the darkness with confidence. God's love for us can be reflected to others as we walk through this mess of a world. Through the Holy Spirit, young and old can discover all that this world has to offer, knowing nothing will change God's presence and promises for us.

Personal Reflection

BIOGRAPHIES

Rosie Adle is a baptized child of God and a lifelong Lutheran. She thanks the Lord for the joys of being home with her dear family, helping at church, being outside, and caring for others in Christian love. She teaches online deaconess classes for Concordia Theological Seminary, Fort Wayne. Deaconess Adle lives in Imperial, Nebraska, just down the street from Zion Lutheran Church, where the Adle family loves to spend much of their time.

Alli Bauck identifies as a busy but blessed stay-at-home mom. She is a lifelong Lutheran and native of Olathe, Kansas, where she lives with her husband and three little boys. In her (rare) spare time, she enjoys napping, catching up with loved ones, and crafting. Alli is also an active author and contributor to Lutheran Women in Mission (LWML), Visual Faith™ Ministry, and Next Step Press.

Terri Bentley writes Bible studies and devotions in the Idaho mountains where she lives with her husband and two big dogs. After raising three children and retiring as a high school English teacher, she is now under contract to publish a historical romance series about Lutheran immigrants. Terri maintains a devotional blog at mountainpraises.blogspot.com and chairs the LWML Christian Resource Editors Committee. When she is not writing, she likes to kayak with her grandchildren or work jigsaw puzzles.

Amy Bird is a World Vision editor and CPH author on Christian living (read more from Amy in the quarterly *Lutheran Life* magazine!). She studied communication and theology at Concordia University Wisconsin and holds an MA in systematic theology from Concordia Seminary. Amy lives in Illinois with her husband, Aaron, who serves as a pastor.

Janine Bolling is a transformative student and community engagement specialist from Brooklyn, New York, serving as executive director of Our Saviour Lutheran School in the Bronx. Deaconess Bolling holds a BA in theology and an MA in public administration and is currently an EdD student at CUW. She is an online adjunct and course designer at Maryville University in St. Louis and at Concordia St. Paul.

Rachel Bomberger is a writer, editor, home educator, cohost of *The Lutheran Ladies' Lounge* podcast for KFUO Radio, and regular online contributor to *The Lutheran Witness*. A graduate of Concordia University, Ann Arbor, she also holds an MA in English from Indiana University—Purdue University, Fort Wayne. She enjoys reading, gardening, and spending time with her Navy chaplain husband and their four beautiful children.

Jessica Bordeleau is an author, speaker, and media producer who develops tools that point to Jesus. Jessica holds a BA in education and an MA in systematic theology and has spent more than a decade working with youth and young adults. She loves photography, nature, and spending time with her husband and their three children. She is passionate about creative ways to share the love of Christ!

Jessica Brashear is the K–8 school counselor for St. John Lutheran School in Seward, Nebraska. She is the program developer and former director of the Master of Arts in school counseling program at Concordia University, Nebraska, and is currently serving as adjunct faculty. She is passionate about combining mental health awareness and school counseling with the hope of Jesus.

Elizabeth Bruick is a wife, mother of three adult children, and author of two children's books and two devotionals. From California to Ohio, she has enjoyed leading Bible studies and retreats, hospitality, working a variety of jobs, and getting to know the people and culture of the cities she and her DCE husband have lived in. If you can't find her, she'll be cooking, baking, or hanging out with family.

Deb Burma is a sought-after speaker for women's conferences, retreats, and ministry events. Her books include *JOY: A Study of Philippians*, *Living a Chocolate Life*, and *Be Still & Know: A Study of Rest and Refuge*. Deb is a pastor's wife, mom, blogger, and coffee/chocolate connoisseur. Above all, she is a grace-filled child of God.

Rebekah Curtis is a housewife, church lady, and school mom. She has been an essayist for websites including The American Conservative, Public Discourse, First Things, and The Federalist; and magazines including *Touchstone*, *Chronicles*, *Salvo*, and *Lutheran Forum*. She is coauthor of *LadyLike: Living Biblically*. She and her husband have eight children.

Heather Choate Davis is an LA-based author, speaker, theologian, liturgist, songwriter, and spiritual director. She has her MA in theology from Concordia University Irvine. In 2020, she released her first album—*Life in the Key of God*—sixteen months after her first piano lesson. Find out more at heatherchoatedavis.com.

Connie Denninger is a family life educator and the cofounder of Visual Faith® Ministry, having studied the impact of social media in the spiritual formation of women. She loves beauty in the sacred space of home and hosting Creative Haven visual arts events. Spending time with her ten grandchildren and gardening are both delights. She and her husband, John, love leading tours to Israel and Greece.

Michelle Diercks is a speaker, host of the *Peace in His Presence* podcast, Bible teacher, and women's ministry leader. She is the author of *Promised Rest: Finding Peace in God's Presence.*

Caitlin May Dinger is a director of Christian education with twenty-five years of experience in congregational and outdoor ministries. She and her husband, Andrew, a pastor, are blessed to be the parents of three boys. Caitlin enjoys gardening and home preserving, all things Jane Austen, and photography. Her life is powered by a lot of forgiveness and a lot of coffee.

Molly Dixon is a mis-organized, fly-by-the-seat-of-your-pants mother of four and farm wife extraordinaire. She lives on a farm in Pleasanton, Nebraska, with her husband, Pete, and is mostly a stay-at-home mom, although you rarely find her there. You will find her supporting whatever sport her kids are currently in: football, basketball, volleyball, track and field, softball, or baseball. Her family farms and ranches, raising corn, soybeans, cattle, and kids. She is active in LWML at both the district and national levels. Her home is never spotless and the laundry is never done. Molly enjoys dabbling in writing in her spare time.

Faith Doerr is first and foremost a child of God, wife to her high school sweetheart, mother of two, and a mental health coach. Faith currently teaches first grade at Concordia Academy in Omaha, Nebraska, and writes for the blog *Imperfectly Perfect Living.* When she is not teaching and coaching, she loves reading, being outdoors, and sipping chai tea lattes.

Catherine Duerr, author of *Wherever Love May Lead: Your Place in God's Plan,* lives with her husband, Steve, in Bakersfield, California. She thoroughly enjoys her vocation as grandma, and also enjoys writing, exploring, traveling, and spending time with their children.

Margo Heath-Dupre is a wife, mother, educator, and author focused on Bible literacy and helping others apply teachings to everyday life. Church service includes art teacher, principal, seminar leader, LWML national nominating committee, and Heart to Heart—Sisters of All Nations as committee national chair. She is currently serving in cross-cultural ministry and ESL programs and is the author of *Be Thou My Guide: A Bible Study on Trusting God.*

Carol Fedewa is "just a Jesus girl" longing to draw nearer to her Lord. She is a wife and mother who works and volunteers at her church. With a heart tuned to women, she weaves threads of faith, God's Word, and encouragement into social media posts for her church's women's ministry. In her free time, you can find her either walking in nature with her dog or reading a good book and sipping on a steaming cup of tea.

Wendysue Fluegge is a happy wife and mother of two. Her full-time job as a musician has allowed her to visit thirty-one states and the Caribbean, singing about Jesus in churches, hot tubs, parking lots, and flying over Kansas! She's written devotions, themed retreats, and dozens of songs, including "Baby Girl Lullaby," which was published as a children's book with her daughter's illustrations. See more at wendysue.com.

Sharla Fritz is an author, speaker, blogger, musician, and retreat leader. She is also a pastor's wife, mother, grandmother, and lover of resale shops. Sharla and her husband, John, live in a Chicago suburb. She is the author of several books, including *Bless These Lips, Enough for Now, Waiting,* and *God's Relentless Love.*

Perla Gil de Rodriguez is of Mexican descent and was born and raised in Houston, Texas. From 2005 through 2020, she and her husband, Rev. Nelson Rodriguez, served at Comunidad de Gracia, a Hispanic mission church plant in Houston, which later became a multicultural church serving all nationalities with bilingual services. She earned a degree in theological studies through the Center of Hispanic Studies at Concordia Seminary, St. Louis, and was commissioned as a deaconess in 2012. In 2021, Perla accepted a call to serve as deaconess at Gloria Dei Lutheran Church in Houston. There Perla, her husband, and their three children minister together as an integral part of Gloria Dei en Español. She is blessed and thankful to have a family who loves God. With love and grace, she exemplifies the calling of the Great Commission by walking and guiding others to know and believe in Jesus Christ as their Lord and Savior.

Angie Goeke studied psychology and fine arts at Concordia University Austin. She is a singer-songwriter, anti-trafficking activist, part-time middle school art and theater teacher, and part-time director of worship at CrossRoad, Katy, Texas. She's happiest being creative and playing board games with her family.

Heidi Goehmann is a licensed clinical social worker and mental health care provider, theologian, writer, and advocate. Heidi can always be found at heidigoehmann.com, which provides resources and advocacy for mental health, genuine relationship, and hope for each day. She lives in Michigan with her husband, four kids, and 1.5 dogs.

Noemi Guerra is the program director for Hispanic ministry at Lutheran Hour Ministries, where she is a podcast writer and cohost. She also works for the Texas District (LCMS). Noemi has written for *Portals of Prayer, Portales de Oración,* and *Lutheran Mission Matters* and has served for more than twenty years across the LCMS. She earned a BA in human relations and justice studies from the University of Iowa and graduated from the deaconess program at Concordia Seminary, St. Louis, where she also earned her MA in practical and systematic theology. The daughter of Panamanian missionaries, she and her husband, Lincon (a pastor), have two sons and a daughter. They live in Lubbock, Texas.

Sarah Gulseth is a baptized child of God and certified #hymnnerd, living in St. Louis with her husband, Luther, and kitties Mandy and Vader. She is the digital media specialist for KFUO Radio, cofounder and cohost of *The Lutheran Ladies' Lounge* podcast and community, and is cohost of *The Coffee Hour.* She is a proud Michigander and alum of Concordia University Chicago who loves enjoying the vibrant beauty of God's creation.

Hannah Hansen is a writer and content marketing specialist at an advertising agency in Michigan, where she lives with her husband, a pastor, and their golden retriever. When she's not working, you'll find her running outside, cooking new vegan recipes, or shopping at the thrift store.

Lindsay Hausch loves mentoring women, supporting and partnering with her husband (a full-time pastor), and staying home with her three littles. In her cracks of free time, she devours books and wrestles to write meaningful words. A popular blogger and social media influencer, Lindsay is the author of *Take Heart: God's Comfort for Anxious Thoughts.* Follow her at lindsayhausch.com or find her on social media; she loves making new friends.

Pa Her is a Hmong-American who grew up in the bustling city of Milwaukee, Wisconsin. Pa considers her faith and family to be most important to her. A lifelong learner, she studied elementary education at the University of Wisconsin-Milwaukee and currently teaches second grade. As a self-professed homebody, she enjoys spending time with her five kids, reading, and fellowshipping with close friends. Pa and her family live in St. Louis, Missouri, where her husband, Joel, is attending seminary.

Christina Hergenrader is an author and speaker. Her published books include *God Loves Moms, Love Rules: A Study of the Ten Commandments, Family Trees & Olive Branches, Shine: Reflecting God's Love, Inspired by the Holy Spirit,* and *Last Summer at Eden.* She is wife to Mike and mom to four beautiful teens. She loves to spend time at the beach with her rescue greyhounds.

Sarah Holtan is an authentic speaker, author, and advocate. She currently serves as the special advisor to the president and professor of communication at Concordia University Wisconsin and Ann Arbor. Her first career was in the media, producing live television news on the ABC affiliate in Milwaukee. Sarah earned a PhD in journalism education from Marquette University, an MS in education from Concordia University Wisconsin, and a BA in mass communication and political science from Augsburg College. She lives in the Milwaukee area with her two children.

Martha Streufert Jander, writer, author, and editor, has taught in various congregations and served as an editor at CPH. With a master's degree in early childhood, she is also a trained Stephen Minister. Mother of five adult children and "Oma" to thirteen grandchildren, Martha and her husband, Lou, respond to people's spiritual needs after disasters through their CrownPoint Ministries.

Rehema Kavugha is serving at Lutheran Church Extension Fund as the director of synod relations and has been serving at LCEF since May 2019. A graduate of Concordia University Nebraska, Rehema received a bachelor's degree in K–12 music, a BFA in vocal music, and in 2019 earned an MBA. She lives with her trusty sidekick of fourteen years, her dog Skittles.

Haleh Kersten serves as the executive director of LINC Austin Outreach in Austin, serving individuals experiencing homelessness. She has been married to her best friend, Kevin, for more than twenty-five years, and they are proud parents of two sons. Her family is her greatest joy. She is renewed by anything involving the outdoors and loves music and reading.

Katie Koplin studied communications at Bethany Lutheran College in Mankato, Minnesota. She works in her hometown as a substitute teacher, from home as a writer, and loves traveling to speaking engagements. She resides in western Minnesota where hills and trees meet fields of grain. Her husband, Dallas, works as an agronomist, and their four kids love to camp, fish, read, go to all the sports, and play games.

Molly Lackey is a wife, author, and historian. Raised outside of Los Angeles and transplanted to north Alabama her senior year of high school, she was a teenage convert to the Lutheran church who immediately fell in love with the original evangelicals' teachings and history. Molly enjoys drawing, reading, and drinking tea with her husband, Jonathan.

Courtney Limmer is a DCE in the Denver area, where she leads student ministries at Our Father Lutheran Church. She loves exploring new places, playing nerdy games with her husband, Aaron, reading, and drinking tea.

Pat Maier, a former Lutheran educator, enjoys writing, drawing, and speaking to inspire others in their walk with Jesus. Pat is cofounder of Visual Faith Ministry and one of the illustrators of *The Enduring Word Bible*. She loves nature, gardening, and spending time with family in Michigan and Montana. Pat lives in northern Michigan with her husband, Rev. David Maier. They have four children, three kids-in-love, and seven grandblessings.

Tiffany Manor serves as director of The Lutheran Church—Missouri Synod's Life Ministry. After a first career in marketing, Deaconess Tiffany received an MA from Concordia Theological Seminary, Fort Wayne, and earned a DMin from Bethel University. She is married to the Rev. Jonathan Manor; they have five children and two grandchildren.

Megan Mertz is managing editor of *Lutherans Engage the World* magazine and chief copy editor for The Lutheran Church—Missouri Synod. She studied English and art at Valparaiso University and received a master's degree in media communications from Webster University. In her free time, Mertz enjoys reading and traveling.

Cassie Moore is an author, speaker, and the director of next generation ministries at St. Mark Lutheran in Houston, Texas. She is the author of *Authentic Youth Ministry*, contributor to *Connected for Life*, as well as an upcoming historical fiction series and teen devotional. She's published more than eighty articles on youth culture, worked on multiple national and district youth gatherings, and speaks across North America. She is currently pursuing a master's degree in organizational leadership. She and her husband, Pastor Tyler, have two dogs.

Darcy Paape is a called DCE serving at Concordia University Wisconsin as director of the Women's Leadership Institute and as an adjunct professor. As director, she oversees a variety of volunteer work teams to fulfill the institute's mission to educate, encourage, and embolden women in exemplary Christian leadership. Darcy is passionate about young adults, mentoring, and providing tools for emerging Christian leaders. Darcy is the author of *Someone to Walk With: A Woman's Guide to Christian Mentoring*. She lives in Grafton, Wisconsin, with her husband, Adam, and two daughters.

Kristina Paul serves as the connections coordinator at Concordia Lutheran Church in Kirkwood, Missouri, leads women's ministry, and supports families with children who have special needs. She played basketball and volleyball at Drake University, where she graduated with a degree in psychology and business. She was a social worker and youth director before earning an MA in theology and her deaconess certification at Concordia Seminary. She and her husband, Nate, have three children and one large goofball of a dog named Oakley.

Kathy Pingel studied elementary education/church teacher and music at Concordia University, St. Paul. She is the director of women and family ministries at St. Paul's Lutheran, Janesville, Wisconsin. Her happy place is time spent with family, walking her puppy, creating memories in the kitchen, and sharing God's Word with women.

Raquel A. Rojas is the deaconess of Redeemer Evangelical Lutheran Church in the Bronx, New York. She received an MA in deaconess studies from Concordia Theological Seminary, Fort Wayne, and received her clinical education at Calvary Hospital in the Bronx (ACPE). Raquel is a district president for Lutheran Women in Mission (LWML). Grateful for all our Lord's gifts, Raquel loves to laugh and enjoys traveling.

Heather Ruesch has a background in child development and psychology with more than fifteen years as an educator. The author of *Sexuality Mentality*, she is a professional speaker for assemblies, retreats, and workshops specializing in the topics of human dignity, depression and anxiety, and pro-life issues. She is a pastor's wife, mother of three, and founder of the You Matter Tour™, an ongoing speaking tour that has reached thousands of teens with a message that transforms the way they see and approach themselves and others (youmattertour.org). Heather has a deep love of health, wellness, and pizza.

Sarah Schultz studied Lutheran elementary education at Concordia University Wisconsin. She currently teaches middle school math at St. John's Lutheran Elementary and Middle School in West Bend, Wisconsin. She speaks, trains, and presents for Dignity Revolution and is passionate about authentic relationships, cultivating the potential in others, and Kingdom work.

Barbara Shippy is a wife, mom, and writer. In 2019, she launched simquily.com as a platform to share her thoughts—and those of others—about the simple and quiet life. A graduate of the Missouri School of Journalism at the University of Missouri, Barbara formerly worked as a copywriter and editor. She and her family live in St. Louis, Missouri.

Julianna Shults is a self-proclaimed nerd, coffee snob, and obsessive aunt. She currently serves as program manager of resource and leadership for LCMS Youth Ministry. As a director of Christian education with a master's in community development, Julianna has served congregations in Florida and Illinois and now serves the synod in St. Louis. She is coauthor of several CPH books, writes for YouthESource, and cohosts the podcast *End Goals.*

Donna Snow is a multi-published author whose books include *Chosen: A Study of Esther.* She has authored several Bible studies through LWML, some of which have been translated into Russian and Ukrainian. She is a sought-after speaker and author who devotes herself full-time to writing about and sharing the Gospel through her nonprofit ministry, Artesian Ministries. You can connect with Donna at artesianministries.org.

Hannah Van Dellen, writer, preschool teacher, and wife, is the author behind *Loving the Least,* which started as a hobby and has grown into a nationwide blog. A military wife, her husband serves in the U.S. Navy. When she is not teaching, she loves to shop at thrift stores, bake bread, and ride their motorcycle named Millie. You can follow her on Instagram @lovingtheleast and visit her blog at lovingtheleast_.weebly.com.